Foreword

Confession: it took me 18 years to get my memoir published. Many, many times, I thought, "Okay, I guess this isn't going to happen for me." Many, many tears were shed, bathroom floors wet with the slick of them. But something kept pulling back to my story—repeatedly. After finally getting over the most recent rejection, I would sigh and dive back in, trying to find the best way to make my life story and the unexpected plot twists I didn't see coming into an actual book.

Eventually, it worked. But the journey wasn't pretty.

I know there must be authors out there who sit down, type out an entire manuscript without much inner agita in rapid-fire, snag a big-deal agent, sell their book to a publisher at auction, and then coast on the bestseller list. But I don't know any of them. And that's saying something: I've had in-depth, 30-minute conversations on my award-winning daily podcast Moms Don't Have Time to Read Books with more than 1,300 authors.

Every one of them has a story. A tale of perseverance. Failure. Determination. Compulsion. Rebounding. Many have been plagued by self-doubt, imposter syndrome, and deep anxiety. But what separates them from the many writers who never get published and don't come on my show is sheer will. It's the instinct to keep going. To dive back into the manuscript. Revise. Try again. Find a new doorway into the inner sanctum of publishing bliss. That's it. Okay, fine, talent plays a role, too. But it's that indefatigable spirit that turns writers into authors, that deep knowledge that writing, this, THIS, they can do. They can write. And they're not giving up.

For years, I tried to sell my memoir, the heart of which was about losing my best friend on 9/11. I wrote it as a novel, a memoir, another novel. I tried to sell it finished and on proposal, before and after having kids. It wasn't until I thought of the idea of pairing my stories with the books I'd read along the way that Bookends sold. And now, even though it took so long and I faced so much rejection, I get emails every week from readers telling me how much they loved it and that it changed their life. How amazing is that? I could've given up. But I knew I had something to say that others needed to hear. Isn't that why we write? To share and connect? To help and inspire? To move through our words.

After hundreds of hours of author interviews, I decided to start my own publishing company, Zibby Books. Why? I wanted to really put the authors at the center of everything. I didn't want to renovate a publishing house. I wanted to build one from the ground up. How would I structure one to be most collaborative? How could I leverage the connections between authors and team to create the warmest, most welcoming and most supportive culture? I didn't know what I was doing. And I knew it would be hard. But hard doesn't scare me. I partnered with people I trusted and respected who had the deep industry knowledge I needed so I could learn how to run a publishing company.

Now, when I read submitted manuscripts for acquisition, I can't even believe that after all those years, I'm on the other side of the desk. Making or breaking someone's day. I try to read almost everything that comes in, even if it's just a page or two, knowing that it's someone's heart on the line. We only publish contemporary, upmarket fiction and memoir—and only 12 books each year. But those authors—our authors—will be getting the royal treatment. We have to reject most submissions. Many are extremely well-written but just aren't for us. Multiply that by all the houses, and it's clear why writers need thick skins. Publishers have visions of what they want. Knowing that can only help.

You only need one.

You only need one editor, one publisher, to fall in love with your story or to see your potential. That's it! So don't give up until you find the right company. Make sure your proposal and sample chapters are the best they can possibly be. Get a few impartial readers to weigh in and offer suggestions before you submit. Don't blow it by not being prepared. Would you show up to a tennis tournament without practicing?! And then, when your product is ready to go to market, research and find the right home for it and convince them why.

But above all else, do not give up. You have a story to tell. And there's someone out there who is waiting to read it. Someone who needs to hear your story so that they can live a happier life. So think of the reader. Think of the thank-you emails. Motivate yourself to finish the book and just send it in.

So good luck, writer. Here's hoping you sell your book in less than 18 years. In my book, that's speedy.

Warmly,
Zibby Owens
Zibby Owens, CEO and Co-founder, Zibby Books

Zibby Owens is an author, publisher, indie bookstore owner, award-winning podcaster, and CEO. Zibby founded what became Zibby Media in 2018 with her award-winning podcast *Moms Don't Have Time to Read Books*, which now has more than 10 million downloads.

The company (dubbed "the Zibby-verse" by the *L.A. Times*) has since grown to include the publishing house Zibby Books, the magazine Zibby Mag, a virtual and in-person book club Zibby's Book Club, the podcast network Zibby Audio, the education platform Zibby Classes, community events and Zibby Retreats, and a writing community. She recently opened an independent bookstore Zibby's Bookshop in Santa Monica, CA.

Zibby was celebrated as "New York's Most Powerful Book-fluencer" by *New York Magazine*. She's a regular contributor to "Good Morning America" and other print and broadcast outlets - and loves recommending books.

A lifelong reader and writer, Zibby is the author of the memoir *Bookends: A Memoir of Love, Loss, and Literature*, the children's book, *Princess Charming*, the editor of two anthologies, and the upcoming debut novel *Blank* (March 2024).

A graduate of Yale University and Harvard Business School, Zibby lives in New York (and L.A.) with her husband, Kyle Owens of Morning Moon Productions, and her four children. Follow her on Instagram @zibbyowens where she tells it like it is.

www.zibbyowens.com

instagram.com/zibbyowens

twitter.com/zibbyowens

facebook.com/zibbysowens

@zibbyowens

Introduction

According to the Oxford Dictionary, 'publish' means *prepare and issue (a book, journal, piece of music, etc.) for public sale, distribution, or readership.*

From the early days in Mesopotamia with "The Epic of Gilgamesh"—the earliest surviving written literature—through 1492 with the printing of the Gutenberg Bible, publishing evolved through many changes in people and processes. In more recent times, options have ranged from printing your own books (like Walt Whitman) to signing with one of the "Big 5" publishers—and everything in between. We are so fortunate to live in a time when publishing options abound, and authors have more possibilities than ever before to get their manuscripts into the hands of readers.

When Grace Sammon floated the idea of a three-book series focusing on writing, publishing, and marketing a book, I was beyond thrilled to partner on a project bringing together so many talented industry writers and professionals who offer inspiration, insights, and information on the very topics that keep authors up nights with worry, provide conversational fodder for writing groups, and give birth to creativity far beyond the written page. I was excited about the volume focusing on publishing, with the opportunities it offers to learn from amazing powerhouses in the publishing world and share them with our readers. From the first words of the foreword by Zibby Owens—author, influencer, and CEO of Zibby Enterprises—we are encouraged along our own journey, which will inevitably lead to many challenges, as well as a need for patience and flexibility in dealing with detours along the way. Keep turning the page, and our talented contributors have risen to the challenge of escorting us along this path. From Brooke Warner of *She Writes Press*, writing about new paths in publication, to Natalie Obando, who strives to include new voices into our publishing world, each chapter brings a fresh outlook, new ideas to embrace, and plans to put into place along your own publishing journey. Whether that journey leads to self-publishing, like Wilnona Marie (whose journey led to radio and podcasting to empower other authors) or sending queries to agents like Sarah Bullen (who shares insights and tips to get your query read), the pages of this book have powerful insights and tools to share with writers on many different paths, with all paths leading to publication.

Each contributor has their own unique point of view, and hail from locations around the globe, so you will find a variety of styles and approaches to publishing within these pages. When we decided upon a three-book series—focusing upon writing, publishing, and marketing—one major challenge was determining exactly where one book would end and the next begin, as there is a lot of 'grey area' between those stages. Thus, you will find chapters here that could also have been placed in *Launch Pad: The Countdown to Writing Your Book*—such as topics on editing and diversity in writing—as well as some which touch upon our next stage of marketing. We have also included topics which may appeal to some writers but not necessarily all books, such as chapters on audiobooks and illustrations. Take a look through the pages, and I'm sure you will find the pearls of wisdom and encouragement you are seeking and that aligns with your own path and plans.

There are as many paths to publication as there are books to be published, no two paths—even those seemingly on the same road—are exactly alike. And with options ranging from the author having total control (along with total responsibility!) to teams of professionals guiding a book to publication, no one method is the right fit for every author—or even every book. Along my own journey, as CEO of Red Penguin Books (and all the rest) for the past 17 years I have been delighted to meet hundreds of authors and support them on a variety of publication paths. The result is that authors often select different paths for different books, as the author recognizes the need for a new approach that is a better fit for that particular book. I have been inspired by the many publishers I have met—each passionate about their own processes as they strive to empower others through publication. And of course, I have enjoyed reading the fruits of publication—from *The Joy of Cooking* which was originally self-published and sits proudly in my kitchen—to books delivered wirelessly from the world's largest publishing houses to my tablet while I lie on the sofa.

My own journey as a publisher began with my most important publication to date—the memoir dictated by my beloved step-father to my mother when he was suffering from Alzheimer's. *Time Was* has sold eight copies—plus the ones I had printed to distribute to our family—so that a man who will never meet his future generations here on Earth will nonetheless be known and loved by his family to come. They can read about him growing up poor in Manhattan, being injured in World War II, receiving one of the first cornea transplants ever, and over-coming all to open an advertising agency on Madison Avenue. His story—and yours—deserve the power of publication, and I am grateful every day for my part in bringing those stories to the world.

Bellerose Village, New York
April 2023
RedPenguinBooks.com

The Forked Road to Publishing Your Novel
Betty Lee Crosby

For an author, there are few things as exciting as seeing your book in the front window of Barnes & Noble or on the USA Today Bestseller List. It's a thrill that rivals the birth of your first child. Every author aspires to that kind of success, but only a few make it. The difference between those who don't and those who do is often an understanding of how the publishing industry actually works. There is no one road to success, there are many roads, each with its own potholes and hazards. I've watched the publishing industry go through a multitude of changes, and I've had to change along with it. I hope that by sharing some of my experiences, I can enrich yours and make your journey to success a bit easier.

When I first began writing fiction, eBooks were not even a blip on the horizon. It was 2004, three years before Amazon introduced the Kindle and six years before eBooks would outsell hardcovers. When I began my journey, I thought the key to success was simply writing a good book. With over a decade of experience in writing for business, I felt reasonably confident that I could sit down at the computer and crank out a bestseller. That was mistake number one.

Writing business articles meant sticking to the facts, the what, where, and when. There was no need for dramatic scene-setting or soul-stirring emotion. Fiction was diametrically different. With fiction, it wasn't enough to simply tell the reader how the character felt, you had to show them. You had to create a world where the reader experienced what the character was experiencing. This was not an easy transition for me. It took almost two years, and I didn't do it alone. I joined a writer's group at the local library and experienced critiques that sometimes felt unfair. Still, I returned, week after week. Listening to members of the group read aloud, my ear became attuned to things I hadn't noticed before. As I continued to write, I set aside time at the end of each day to read what I'd written aloud. When I stumbled over a word, I knew it was because it didn't belong there. When a character's voice sounded unrealistic, I dug deeper into my own emotions and forced myself to feel what the character was feeling. I devoured the books that everyone was talking about and those that topped the bestseller lists. As I read, I studied what made the characters interesting or likable and what moved the story forward. I wrote more words than I could possibly count and completed two novels before having a third that I believed was good enough to warrant publishing. When my manuscript for *The Twelfth Child* won First Place for unpublished fiction in an American Pen Women literary competition, I figured I was ready to enter the publishing world. At that point, I could almost see my name on *The New York Times* bestseller list and began wondering who'd star in the movie.

I am by nature a goal-setter. My goal was to write a good story, send it off to a publisher, and wait for the royalties to roll in. I bought a Directory of Literary Agents, selected the ones best suited to represent my novel, and began sending out query letters. It came as a rude awakening to learn those agents were not waiting for my novel to land on their desks. In fact, they were not the least bit interested. Despite my award-winning manuscript and a query letter that I felt certain would knock their socks off, I received enough rejections to wallpaper a good-sized bedroom.

Some agents replied with nothing more than a pre-printed post-card saying thanks, but no thanks. Others took time to person-alize a form letter, and a handful actually expressed a liking for the book but passed because I had no platform.

Platform? I hadn't the foggiest idea of what a platform was.

Lesson number one—show the world how interesting you are before you start to market your work. I learned the hard way that a platform is the number of followers you have, the people who have shown an interest in you and your work. Publishers are impressed by numbers. They want to know there are people out there waiting to hear what you have to say. They count the number of Twitter followers, Facebook fans, Instagram likes, TikTok shares, and such. That's your platform, your potential fan base. It doesn't matter that you have yet to publish your first book, you have followers who will be ready to buy it when you do. The days of a starving artist hunkered down in an attic loft to write the next great American novel are long gone. We are living in an age where social media is the gas that drives your awareness engine.

Despite the ever-growing number of rejections, I continued to write and was working on a fourth novel when a friend told me about the company that had agreed to publish her book. Sidestepping the need for an agent, she'd gone directly to the publisher. Since it was not one of the well-known publishing houses, I expressed concern that it was a vanity press—one where you pay to have your book published. Pushing aside any lingering apprehension, I sent my award-winning manuscript along with my not-yet-successful query letter. They responded almost immediately, offering me an exclusive seven-year contract on both the hardcover and paperback versions of the book with a one-dollar advance. In exchange, I would receive a modest royalty on every book sold. Once I finished dancing around the room to celebrate my success, I signed the contract and sent it back. Foolish girl. Lesson number two, investigate the company and make sure you know the questions to ask before signing a contract.

A few months later, the book was released at $19.95, which was overpriced for a paperback, but there was little I could do about it. While I had creative input on the cover design and editing, the publisher controlled marketing, distribution, and pricing.

Having now learned the value of a platform, I focused on building one. I chatted on Facebook morning, noon, and night. Friended everyone I knew, as well as strangers who had absolutely no interest whatsoever in me or my book, and joined any number of writing groups. I also booked speaking engagements at women's clubs, libraries, and coffee houses. Before long, my hard work began to pay off. The book started selling fairly well with the paperback ranked somewhere about 10,000 on Amazon. That's when I came face to face with the consequences of ignoring Lesson Number Two.

The publisher upped the price of the paperback to a whopping $24.95. Now we are talking about a paperback book from a somewhat unknown author. The price was ridiculous. I argued that not even John Grisham could sell a paperback at that price, but it was to no avail. The price remained at $24.95. In all good conscience, I couldn't ask people to pay that for a paperback, so I stopped promoting the book. My plan was to continue writing, wait for the contract to expire, then sell the book to a more reputable publishing house.

I was back to querying literary agents when one of the writers in my group suggested a print-on-demand company. They had the capability to drop ship the books to bookstores and make them available on Amazon. This was my first foray into what would eventually become the monumental world of self-publishing. Lesson number three—think outside the box.

That firm was called Instant Publisher, and that's exactly what they did. The print quality was good, and I could earn considerably more than the piddling royalty I was given on the first book. The big change was that I had to provide finished artwork for the book's interior and cover. With all of the formatting tools and design programs available today, this is virtually a no-brainer, but back then it was a big deal. I had an ad agency do the cover design for *Cracks in the Sidewalk* and repaid them with copywriting work, then muddled through the text layout myself. The interior was done in Microsoft Word, but it took forever and had more mistakes than I care to admit.

This is where the story gets interesting. That tiny little eBook blip suddenly exploded. Sony released an electronic reader in 2006, and a year later Amazon introduced both the Kindle and KDP, a program that enabled authors to upload files and publish their own books. Before the decade was out, the publishing world was forever changed.

Authors could now control their own fate—with or without a literary agent. Every phase of bringing a book to market could be handled by the authors themselves. This included formatting and cover design. True, there was a somewhat steep learning curve in using these wonderful new technical capabilities, but wasn't that to be expected? In exchange for wrangling your way through pre-set margins and Mobi formatting your eBook earned a monumental 70% royalty. Compare that to the paperback's 10-15% royalty.

As the popularity of eBooks grew, the greedy publisher who priced my paperback at $24.95 took notice. *The Twelfth Child* was now in year three of a seven-year contract. They contacted me and asked that I sign a release giving them the right to publish the eBook version. Well, you know the old adage, fool me once shame on you, fool me twice shame on me—of course, I refused to sign it. We went back and forth a number of times, then they finally offered me the option of buying back my contract. I jumped at the chance to do so.

Back then there was no Bent Pine Publishing, there was only me. Me, struggling to learn formatting while I was editing *Spare Change*. Me, looking at this great big opportunity sitting in front of me. Being an author was my second career, one I came to after over two decades in marketing. I considered myself semi-retired. I was writing novels because I had stories to tell. I was simply doing what I loved to do. Did I really want to tackle this giant bear all alone?

My husband had absolutely no interest in the book biz. He was a Wall Street guy who could discuss stocks and bonds for hours on end, but his eyes glazed over when I talked about a weak protagonist or chapter setup. He had however mentioned retire-ment—not completely, but partially, perhaps with a business where he could put in a few hours a day and still manage a round of golf.

I suggested he consider being a literary agent or publisher and he frowned. As I segued into explaining the different ways he could help me, his expression didn't change. So, I changed my approach and began talking about the huge opportunity of a business that was still in its infancy. He's a man who loves a chal-lenge, and this piqued his interest. Although he was thumbs down on the thought of being an agent, he did see a glimmer of potential in publishing. A glimmer was enough for me.

Alone, I was an author struggling to find my place in this rapidly evolving book industry. Now, with a business-minded partner on board, we became a company. Bent Pine Publishing was set up as an S-corporation, and everything was housed under that umbrella. My books were registered with Bowker, ISBN numbers were purchased in lots of ten, an actual bookkeeping system replaced my sticky notes, the horrendous job of formatting was outsourced to a professional formatter who actually knew what she was doing, and I went back to writing.

There's a lesson to be learned here, but it's not necessarily needing a partner to build a business. It's structuring yourself as a business. The investment in professional editing, good cover design, and clean formatting can be an individual decision well worth the cost. The same is true of a workable bookkeeping system. Don't make the mistake of thinking you have to do everything yourself. Be resourceful, and build a team of freelance professionals. They will give you what you need when you need it and without the burden of a salaried staff.

If your heart is set on being with a traditional publisher, go for it. Write a query letter that will have them begging to read the book, and don't limit yourself to querying agents. Look beyond the Big Five, and try a direct approach with some of the smaller, more specialized companies. Signing with a traditional publisher means you've got a partner to share some of the heavy lifting. You'll have an editor committed to seeing you succeed, developmental advice to plug the holes in your story, and professional proofreaders, designers, and marketing experts—all with an eye to making you and your book shine. A traditional publisher can open doors you cannot open on your own, and they can get widespread distribution of your book to both bookstores and libraries. But there's a caveat, unless you're already a superstar you will be expected to do much of the marketing yourself, and you will most definitely need a platform. Signing with a traditional publisher eliminates your up-front costs for design and formatting, but the royalty rate is almost always lower, particularly on eBooks. A lower royalty rate does not necessarily mean lower earnings. If your book sells well, the royalty rate is easily offset by expanded distribution and greater sales volume.

Traditional publishing is not the only road to success. While self-publishing was once the red-headed stepchild of the industry, it is now recognized as a highly profitable way for independent-minded authors to take control of their destiny. Most traditional houses limit an author to one, perhaps two books a year. Self-publishing enables you to decide how many or how few books to publish. You control the schedule, distribution channels, pricing, and every phase of design and development.

Whether you are a first-time author testing the water with an eBook, or a mid-lister publishing both paperback and hardcover versions, let's look at what the process involves. We'll start by assuming you now have a finished manuscript; this is where you need to stop and ask yourself, has it been professionally edited? Some authors can also be good editors, but editing your own work is virtually impossible. Your eye doesn't see what is on the page, it sees what you intended to write. I cannot stress strongly enough the importance of a well-edited book. You might not see those mistakes, but your readers will, and they'll mention them in their reviews. Once your manuscript is truly ready for publishing, you can choose to go one of two routes, the easiest being to hire professionals to do the design and formatting. There are any number of freelance formatters who can turn your manuscript into a ready-to-upload file in days and for a very moderate cost. The same is true for cover design, but designers can be costly, so ask for an estimate before moving ahead.

When you are looking for a cover designer or formatter, search out books that have a look and feel similar to what you want, then check the copyright page to see if those contributors are credited. If you are part of a writing community, ask around; find out which designers and formatters your colleagues are using, or join an online writer's group and start up a conversation. You'll be amazed at how much you can learn from fellow authors. We are all beginners at some point, and the authors who have blazed a trail before you are usually quite willing to share what they have learned.

Your second option is to do everything yourself. This may sound a bit overwhelming, but given today's technology it is easier than you might think. Vellum is a user-friendly formatting program that features pre-made book designs. You can download Vellum for free, play with it, and decide whether or not it's for you. You don't pay for the program until you are ready to actually export a book, then there is a one-time cost that is under $300. Book Brush is a design program with loads of learning tutorials, countless typefaces to choose from, and thousands of stock photos. The program contains numerous pre-made cover designs, 3-d options, and a variety of ready-to-use layouts for marketing materials such as ads, banners, and posts. Book Brush has an annual subscription charge, but in my estimation, it is well worth the money.

Okay, now that you have an awesome cover design and properly formatted interior files, you are ready to go. You have two major distribution channels and both of those have multiple options. Since eBooks now account for a substantial portion of all book sales, let's look at some of those options. If this is your first venture and you are looking to establish a start-up reader base, you might want to consider Amazon's Kindle Select program. The advantage here is that in addition to selling your book on their website, Amazon allows their Kindle Unlimited subscribers to read your book for free and you get paid for every page read. Having a read-for-free book can sometimes make it easier for an unknown author to establish a reader base and get some of those all-important reviews. The program, however, does have its limitations. Putting your book in the Kindle Select program requires a three-month term of exclusivity. You must agree not to sell or give away your eBook to any other retailer or distribution source for that period of time. After the initial three-month term, you have the option of canceling your Select enrollment or renewing it. This exclusivity does not include your paperback or hardcover books, you are free to market those formats to other retailers while enrolled in the Select program.

A more aggressive alternative is to set up wide distribution for your eBook. This approach makes your books available on Amazon, Barnes & Noble, Kobo, Google Play, and Apple Books. There are pros and cons to this approach. To maximize the effectiveness of wide distribution, you will want to customize your files for each retailer—ask for a review posted to that site, add buy links for your other books, and include a sign-up for your newsletter. Each of these retailers offers its own promotional opportunities, take advantage of them, and make yourself and your book visible on that site. With wide distribution, your opportunity for growth is far greater, but it requires a good deal more time and management. If you are working with a professional formatter, you can most likely have them upload the file and enter the metadata for each of those retailers. You will pay for their time but save on yours.

Although your eBook will likely be the biggest money-maker in your publishing portfolio, getting your book into bookstores means you will also need a print version. The production process for either a paperback or hardcover is much the same as it is for an eBook. Here again, you need customized interior and cover files. If you have an eye for design and the technological skills, you can create these yourself, or you can do as I have done and have your cover designer and formatter give you ready-to-upload print files.

Lightning Source is a one-and-done print-on-demand resource. Once you've uploaded your files, your book will be listed in their catalogue and made available to bookstores and libraries. You will also be able to bulk-order quantities of books for your own use. A word of advice here—if you are setting yourself up as an independent publishing company, use your own ISBN numbers rather than one provided by Lightning Source. ISBN numbers can be purchased directly from Bowker, and you will need a different number for each version of the book—eBook, paperback, or hardcover—but the ISBN for each version can be used for all distribution vendors.

When I published my first book there were very few options, now there are countless roads to success. Your publishing experience can be as big or small as you want it to be. You no longer have to travel the traditional publishing route, you can be a start-up independent, self-published author, or a hybrid combination. The choice is yours. Be fearless. Explore the pros and cons of various alternatives. Ask questions. And, if partway down the road you find you've made a mistake, don't be afraid to switch.

Top 10 Countdown

Before you take that first step on your road to becoming a successful author, here are a few of my favorite tips for success.

10. Make yourself a brand. Start building your platform immediately. Set up your Facebook, Instagram, Twitter, and TikTok pages under your own name or the pseudonym you plan to use. Remember that first book will probably not be your last.

9. Make your debut novel a gem. You only get one chance to make a first impression, so before you hit the 'publish' button, make sure that story is ready to be read. Polish the manuscript until it shines. Read the book aloud to find the lumpy transitions and cut the extraneous words.

8. Make certain your work is properly edited, not by your mom or Aunt Bessie, but by a professional who will double-check your timeline, and catch those pesky typos, repeated words, and errors.

7. Join an online writer's group and take part in the conversations. You'll be amazed at how much you can learn from one another. A big bonus in doing this is that you can build relationships that will remain with you throughout your publishing journey.

6. Never try to write to market. The market changes quickly, and while WW2 stories may be hot today, they can easily be passé tomorrow. Find your own voice; for example, write the stories you were meant to write.

5. If you go the route of an independent, own your work. Purchase and apply your own ISBN numbers. Keep everything under the same umbrella, whether it is your company name or your own.

4. Set up a website and post periodic blog articles relevant to the book you are writing. If you are tech-savvy, set up keywords to maximize your Search Engine Optimization. If you need help, hire a pro. The right SEO can have your name popping up when anyone Googles the subject you're writing about.

3. Create a newsletter and build a mailing list. The people who sign up to receive your newsletter will be your best fan base. They are the ones you can reach out to with news of a new book, a sales promotion, or a review request.

2. Use front and back matter links in your eBook to drive readers to your website, and social media pages. And as you release additional books update the back matter to include teaser excerpts and buy links to the newer books.

1. Respect your readers. Thank them for reviews. Answer them when they message you on Facebook or Instagram. Let them know how much you appreciate their support. And, if heaven forbid, someone does post a less than favorable review—never approach them about it, or argue the point. Take their critique for what it's worth, then move on.

Meet Betty Lee Crosby

Bette Lee Crosby is the USA Today bestselling author of twenty-four novels and recipient of numerous literary awards. Often hailed as a masterful storyteller, her novel *Baby Girl* was named Best Chick Lit of 2016 by Huffington Post and her 2019 release *Emily, Gone* won the International Book Award for Women's Fiction. Her most recent release is *The Fault Between Us*, a historical novel based on a true story. Crosby, a lover of dogs and all things Southern, laughingly admits to being a night owl whose guilty pleasure is late-night chats with fans and friends on social media.

Website: https://betteleecrosby.com

Facebook: https://www.facebook.com/authorbetteleecrosby

Instagram: https://www.instagram.com/betteleecrosby/

Goodreads:

http://www.goodreads.com/author/show/
3222582.Bette_Lee_Crosby

Working with Editors in the Publishing Process

Robb Grindstaff

Writing a novel is complicated. It's like making a movie. There are hundreds of moving parts, dozens of characters, and hundreds of different aspects of both the art and the craft.

But a movie has an entire crew. A novel has one author. You are the screenwriter, the director, the producer, and the camera operator. You're the gaffer and the grip, and no one even knows what those jobs are.

An editor can be an integral part of your film crew, helping keep all the parts moving in the right direction. An editor can be your "best boy"—another rarely understood film job.

I know what you're thinking. Who needs an editor? What is an editor? When do I hire an editor? Where do I find a good one? How long does editing take and, most importantly, how much does it cost? Let alone, why do I need another editor now that my book is finished and it's at the publisher?

Oh, so many questions.

Those questions and more are answered in this step-by-step tutorial on working with *and hiring* the right editor for your novel and knowing what to expect. Let's start with why.

Who Needs an Editor?

Newspapers and news media have reporters who write the stories, and editors who review, critique, and proofread those stories. Book publishing companies have editors who specialize in all the various levels and types of editing. Bestselling authors and world-famous writers have editors.

An objective professional can let you know what is working and what isn't, provide helpful suggestions and constructive criticism, help improve your writing, and develop your style and voice. An editor will catch typos, fix grammar and sentence structure issues, spot continuity issues, and analyze your overall story to see if it is working the way you intended.

You've written a book, and you want people to read it. Not just read but love it. Why would you want to publish or submit an unedited draft?

That's right. You don't.

Every writer needs an editor. Even writers (like me) who are also editors (like me) need editors. No one (not even me; okay, especially not me) can edit their own work. Novice writers need editors. Intermediate writers need editors. Experienced, professional writers need editors. Stephen King has editors. Ernest Hemingway had editors.

Your story is in your head. Your brain processes that story into words on the page. Those words make sense and look right to you because you know the story. No matter how many times you read it, there will be errors—major and minor—that your brain won't see.

- Minor: A missing word. A missing punctuation mark. When you read it, your brain knows it's supposed to be there, so your brain "sees" it.
- Medium: Your character has blue eyes in chapter three. In chapter thirty-seven, she has green eyes. Or you dump a lot of background research into chapter six to explain some phenomenon that is going to be important for readers. But, as an editor might explain, it's dull, boring, interrupts the story for too long, and you will lose readers. An editor will provide you with options to provide readers with the info they need without making their eyes glaze over.
- Major: A plot thread you started in chapter six disappears without a trace or any resolution. Or a character has been described and portrayed as rational, thoughtful, not spontaneous for twenty-nine chapters. Then, in chapter thirty, he does something completely out of character for no explainable reason. A sharp, well-trained outside set of eyes can spot these issues when your brain may not even notice.

But what if I'm submitting to a literary agent? Won't they edit my work?

If you're submitting to literary agents, you want your work to be spotless, engaging, compelling, and professional. Agents get dozens or hundreds of submissions every week. One agent has posted her annual stats on occasion, and they often go something like this:

- Received 10,000 query letters.
- Asked for sample chapters and synopsis from 500; summarily rejected 9,500 queries.
- Asked for full manuscripts from fifty out of the 500 sample chapter submissions.

- Signed two new clients out of the fifty full manuscripts reviewed.
- Only one, or perhaps neither, of those new clients ever receives a contract.

With the volume of queries every agent receives, you want your query letter, your opening chapters, and your full manuscript to be spotless, as well as a compelling story populated with engaging characters. Any little glitch gives the agent a reason to hit the automated email that says thanks but no thanks.

Most literary agents do not provide editing. They expect your submission to be polished and nearly perfect. Editing isn't their job. Helping you become a better writer isn't their job. Their job is to find that one gem in 10,000 and sell it to a publisher.

Give yourself the maximum odds in this numbers game. Every word has to stand out as that of a professional writer who is a master of the art and craft of fiction.

Yes, if you land a contract with a publishing company, they will do even more editing and probably will ask for more revisions. Don't anticipate that you can send an unedited manuscript to an agent, who will sell it to a publisher, and then you can begin edits for the first time. The publisher will send your work through several different types and levels of editing, but if it's not a great well written story, it will never get that far.

But what if I'm self-publishing rather than trying to land an agent?

That's an even tougher assignment. You're going to upload your finished book and sell it directly to the public. You're personally responsible for all the editing processes, including what a team of professionals would do at a publishing company. Do you really want to sell a book that isn't of the top quality you're capable of providing? Would you want to buy one like that? I think not.

It's my first book. I can't afford an editor yet. Once I have some revenue coming in from book sales, I'll hire an editor for my next book.

This is a great way to kill your potential career as an author before it even gets started. If you sell some copies of your first book, not professionally edited, readers notice. They notice the typos, the spelling and punctuation errors. They notice plot holes. They notice that the character's eyes changed color.

And they won't waste their money buying your second book. A handful of bad reviews on your first book can ensure your first and second books won't sell, even if you invest in editing book number two. You want everyone who buys your first book to look forward to your second book, as well as leave positive reviews and tell all their friends about it.

Who needs an editor? You. If you're writing a book, you need an editor.

What is an Editor? What Does an Editor Do? What Do You Mean by 'Different Types of Edits'?

A book editor does a number of different jobs. At the core, an editor serves as your personal writing assistant, instructor, and coach to help you make your story as good as it possibly can be, helps to bring your writing skills to a higher level, and provides advice and techniques that you can apply not to just this book, but to everything you write in the future.

No editor can guarantee your book will be a bestseller or land a high-powered literary agent. No one can promise that. If anyone promises success, run away. And hold onto your wallet.

The editing process is similar, not the same, whether you are with a big house, a small press, or just working independently to make your book the best book possible before it gets into the hands of readers. Typically, an editor will first read your book from start to finish to get an overall impression of the story, characters, narrative arc, character arcs, plot, themes, and general writing skills—strengths and weaknesses.

Then, the editor will read through it again with the proverbial red pen, which today means Microsoft Word, Google doc, or a similar document with 'track changes' mode turned on. The editor will correct errors, smooth out sentences, suggest different word choices, recommend adding a scene, deleting a scene, revising a scene, or rearranging scenes. The editor may have recommendations on how to make your dialogue more realistic and natural, point out a need for more setting and description, or less setting and description. The editor can point out plot holes, narrative arc weaknesses, or weak characterization (two-dimensional characters that readers won't care about). You might have seven characters whose names all start with the letter "J" which can be hard for readers to keep straight. Maybe a character's eyes magically change colors.

> *Side note:* If an editor points out a weakness in your writing or story, that is cause for celebration, not consternation. The editor's job is to find areas that need improvement, along with tips and suggestions on how to do so. Nothing will improve your book more than learning your weaknesses—we all have them—and then learning how to strengthen those areas. This will raise your professional skills for everything you write in the future.

So don't get defensive. The editor is providing you with invaluable input. Of course, just like doctors, some editors may have a smoother bedside manner than others when giving you the not-so-good news about issues that need intervention. But you're looking for the cure, not kindness. Between editors, reviewers, and rejections, a thick skin is a prerequisite in this business.

What do you mean by different types of editing?

There are different types of edits that may be needed at different points in the process. Depending on where you are in your writing journey, you may or may not need all of these. Many freelance editors can provide all of these services. Other editors specialize in one or two of these. If you are independently publishing, you might need to hire different editors for different types of edits. If you are with any of the other types of presses, you may find yourself working with any and all types of editors.

Let's walk through the process from start to finish.

Developmental editing and manuscript analysis/critique

Before you even finish writing the book, or after you've completed a first draft, these are services editors can provide you during the writing process. In addition to a developmental editor or a book coach, you may have worked with writer critique groups and trusted beta readers. This is covered in more detail in Book One of this series, *Launch Pad: The Countdown to Writing Your Book.*

We'll dive into the editing processes after you've finished your manuscript and made it as good as you can.

Line edit

This is what writers usually think about when discussing editing. You submit your finished manuscript to an editor. The editor reads and reviews the entire manuscript. Corrections and suggestions are made in the text, with more suggestions and explanations included in margin comments. The editor will try to catch everything from typos or punctuation errors to plot problems or larger issues, both structural and writing. There may or may not be a separate report that provides more explanation.

Then it's your responsibility to go through every change, accept it, reject it, or revise it in your own way rather than how the editor suggested. It's also your responsibility (and right) to ask questions. Ask for clarification if you don't understand something.

Whether or not the editor does a second pass on your revised manuscript is something you should ask about up front to see if that's included. Know ahead of time what you're getting and what you're paying for.

Copy edit or proofread

A proofreader doesn't get into writing skills, prose style, narrative arc, plot, characterization, or any of the deeper issues. Proofreading is purely to find and correct mistakes. SPAG, it's often called: spelling, punctuation, and grammar.

Proofreading is the final step before sending the polished manuscript off to a literary agent, publisher, or self-publishing.

If you've finished a detailed line edit, after all the editing is done, you still need a proofread. Even though the line edit will catch most errors, it isn't designed to catch them all. And during the back-and-forth editing process, new typos and errors will show up. The editor can make a typo when correcting another thing. Yes, it happens.

Why can't I just run spell check when I'm done revising?

Sure, run spell check and look at everything it flags. But if you meant to type "from" and you typed "form, spell check may not flag it. It's spelled correctly. It's just the wrong word. And grammar-checking software is notoriously difficult. It can be especially difficult in dialogue where you don't want characters to all sound like they are English professors.

You could hire a writing coach to help you through the process, then contract for an analysis/critique of the final draft to see how you need to revise, then pay for a thorough and detailed line edit, with several edits back and forth until you get it just right, then you can hire a proofreader. You might hire the same editor for all of this. Or you might hire different experts for different phases. What is important here is that you understand and follow a process.

You also might find you don't need all of those. If you're a relatively experienced and confident writer, you can finish that first draft, and then polish up a good second or even third draft. Then you might go straight to the line edit and then to a final proofread.

All of those decisions are yours. But realistically evaluate what you need and what your budget is going to be. It cannot be stressed enough, however, that a good editing process separates good books from lesser works.

To recap, the different types of edits are:

- **Line edit:** After you've completed your manuscript and brought it as far as you can. You're confident in your work, but know it needs an outside professional to make it as strong as possible.
- **Proofread:** You've finished your manuscript and had it thoroughly line edited. Now you need a fresh set of eyes to scour it with a fine-tooth comb to look for every typo, SPAG error, and style issue.
- **Submit or publish:** When this proofread is completed, you're ready to send your book out into the world.

Here's an example of actual situations I've encountered. Yes, this has happened more than once:

I've spent the last five years working on my masterpiece novel. It's my first book ever. Now, I'm ready to self-publish. I've set a publication date and ordered thousands of dollars of online ads to promote it and propel me to literary stardom. My launch date is in two weeks. Can you edit it by next Tuesday?

And the answer is . . . (wait for it): No.

If you've spent five years, one year, or six months writing your book, don't rush the editing process in a desire to hurry up and get your book published or into literary agents' inboxes. Allow time to do it right. Why spend that much of your time writing a book and then rush the polishing process? Maybe it needs a total rewrite or significant revisions.

I recommend against using clichés, but don't put the cart before the horse. Don't plan your amazing book launch before it's been thoroughly edited.

There are also some excellent ways to get feedback before you invest in editing, and I highly recommend doing any or all of these:

Self-editing

- Read books on writing fiction. There are tons out there. You can learn a lot of things rather than waiting for an editor to catch them. Learn grammar and sentence structure, verb tenses, fiction-writing techniques, narrative arc, characterization, dialogue, point-of-view, perspective, description, world-building, foreshadowing, flashbacks, and on and on. Learn all you can and put that knowledge to work.
- Take writing courses. Community college, online courses, wherever you can find some instruction. You don't have to go back to the university for an MFA (more power to you if you decide to do this).
- Beta readers. Have a trusted group of writers and avid readers (who may not be writers) read your manuscript and provide you with honest feedback. You will need to

sift through all the feedback to see what makes sense to you and your story, but listen to them carefully.

- In short, find every way you can to improve your writing and story before you hire an editor.

Where Do I Find an Editor?

The best way to find an editor is through other writers, word-of-mouth, and personal experience. If you're in a writers' critique group, ask for recommendations. Ask your social media network.

Do internet searches, but beware. Like any industry, there are lots of scams out there. There are people who love to prey on newbie writers who dream of publication. And there are plenty of well-intended wannabe editors who just don't have the skills, education, training, or experience to do the job you need.

Once you've narrowed down your list to a manageable size, say three to five possibilities, get references. Who else have they edited? What genres do they edit? You don't want to hire a science-fiction editor to edit your southern gothic novel, or a romance editor to handle your horror story, although many editors are quite capable of editing multiple genres.

Contact references and ask questions. How was this editor to work with? How timely? Fair rates and terms? What was the single best piece of advice this editor gave you? Would you hire her again?

Talk to the editor. Maybe a phone call or Zoom, maybe just email. Do you connect? Does she get what you're trying to accomplish? Does she ask good questions about your goals for the book? Does he provide a sample edit at no charge so you can see how he works? Does the editor give you a realistic timeline? Reasonable pricing? How much back-and-forth is included? A time period for follow-up questions?

With a list of reputable editors, reference checks, and a conversation or two, you should be able to find a respected fiction editor with whom you feel comfortable.

How Much Does Editing Cost? How Long Does it Take?

There are numerous factors here, but the only correct answer is "it depends."

What level or type of editing do you need?

- A line editor may be the most expensive as this is the most labor-intensive process.
- Proofreading is usually the least expensive.
- Developmental/writing coach and analysis/critique may fall somewhere in between, depending on how much input you want and how many issues the editor uncovers.

How long is your manuscript?

- This one should be obvious, but all else being equal, a 200,000-word epic saga will cost more than a 40,000-word category romance.

Why does one editor charge more or less than another?

- Pricing often depends on the experience of the editor and their current workload.

How do editors price their services?

- Per word. This is often the best and most common measurement. As this goes to press, it can range from half a cent to five cents per word or more, depending on the complexity and type of edit.

- Per page. Some editors still quote per-page rates, but make sure you know the format they want the document in. You can't just make your manuscript single-spaced, eight-point type with quarter-inch margins and say, "See, it's only seventy-five pages." Calculate 250-300 words per manuscript page. So, you're right back to the per-word rate after all.
- Per hour. Personally, I'd be leery of this. How do you know how many hours the editor will take? How does the editor know? Maybe the editor makes a reasonable estimate based on how complicated the edit will be (based on a sample edit) and the total number of words. So once again, we're back to a per-word rate. You don't want to agree to forty hours of editing, then the editor says, "Well, it took me forty hours to get halfway through, so to finish, I need you to pay for another forty hours."
- A percentage of sales. Unless this is with a hybrid publisher or self-publishing assistance program, steer clear of this as well. With a hybrid publisher, they have an incentive to help you sell as many books as possible, and they may take a percentage of sales for editing services. This can work, but be very clear on the terms in a written contract. For a freelance editor, avoid this arrangement.

The Editorial Freelancers Association (EFA) produces a chart with general ranges of editing rates. Some editors may charge more and some less, but this chart can give you a general guideline for budgeting purposes: https://www.the-efa.org/rates/

- As you can see if you follow the link, proofreading might cost two cents per word, but line editing might cost four cents per word. And many, many good and reputable editors will charge significantly less than these rates.

Budget for it

- Don't "cheap out" on making your book professional and as well-written and polished as possible. If EFA says the average rate for line editing is four cents per word, and somebody says they'll do your 100,000-word manuscript for $100, something is wrong. You'll probably get your money's worth.
- Most expensive doesn't mean the best. If four cents per word is average for line editing, that doesn't mean eight cents per word will get you twice as good of an editor.

Payment arrangements

- Many editors require full payment in advance. Nothing wrong with that—every editor has probably been burned at some point. But make sure it's a reputable and highly recommended editor before forking over your hard-earned cash.
- Some editors (like me) will reserve your spot on the schedule with a partial payment. Then, the balance may be due before work begins, or a second partial payment, with a final payment due when work is completed before the editor sends you the edited manuscript.
- Some editors are much more trusting and will take payment after all the work is done and they've sent you the edited manuscript. These are probably editors who haven't been burned . . . yet. Or, it's an editor you've worked with and with whom you've built a solid, professional relationship.

- Insist on a written contract that spells out all the details of the editing arrangement, including price, timeline, and follow-up.

It's hard to give a timeframe for an edit. Every editor's work pace and schedule are different. Many editors have full-time jobs and edit in their spare time. Some of us do this full-time. We can be booked up months in advance.

In general, with lots of exceptions, I may take a month or more to do one editing pass on an average-size novel. It can depend on what else is going on in life, how long the novel is, how polished the writing is, and how many significant issues I come across.

It might be three months or more before I have an opening in my schedule. Or I might have an opening next week due to a cancellation if another client isn't quite ready.

Editors at Publishing Companies

You've written your book, made it as good as you can on your own, and with the assistance of critique groups and beta readers, then you worked with a freelance editor to improve and polish it to near-perfection. Next, you sent it off to literary agents and publishers, and success! You've landed a publishing contract.

Guess what you get to do now?

Edit and revise some more.

Your publisher, whether a major publishing house, a small press, or a hybrid publisher, will assign an editor to you to go through it again. And you'll be asked to make more changes.

Your goal here is just like with a freelance editor. Build a rapport, a relationship, a trusted bond with that editor. The editor's single most important job is to make your book great. Even greater than it already is, and if you've landed a publishing contract, it's pretty great already.

You don't want to get the reputation at a publishing house as "that writer," the one who is difficult to work with, who insists your writing is divinely inspired and can't be changed. If you want to publish more than one book, you want to be that writer who knows how to work with an editor professionally and collegially. You both have the same end result in mind.

That doesn't mean you can't ask questions or stick up for yourself and your story. But pick your battles. If the editor wants you to delete or change something that you believe is important to your story, discuss it. Explain what you're trying to accomplish. Maybe the editor will have a better suggestion. Sometimes even editors will change their minds and agree with you.

There will be back-and-forth line edits, more proofreading, and then galley proofs. Then advance review copies.

And guess what? You're likely to spot errors at every step. Your 100,000-word novel probably has half a million letters, characters, and spaces. Something invariably slips into the final printed, hardbound copy of your book.

We editors like to remain mysterious sometimes. When it comes to working with editors and getting a manuscript fit for publication, there are a lot of questions to consider. Hopefully, this chapter provided some answers to help clear up the mystery. Your mission is to find an editor you're comfortable with, who understands your goals and your story, and who has the skills to help you bring your book to the next level. Ideally, you will have a long-term relationship with an editor who will help guide and further your career.

Top 10 Countdown

10. Research and select a reputable editor that is a good fit, one with whom you can build a long-term relationship.

9. Get feedback for free from beta readers and critique groups before investing in an editor.

8. Do advance self-editing by learning all you can about the art and craft of writing fiction.

7. Allow time for the editing process.

6. Budget for editing.

5. Understand the different types of edits.

4. Determine what type of editing you need.

3. Understand what editors do.

2. Editing is an integral part of writing a book, not an option.

1. If you are a writer, you need an editor.

Meet Robb Grindstaff

In addition to a career as a journalist, newspaper editor, publisher and media executive, Robb Grindstaff has written fiction most of his life. The newspaper biz has taken him and his family from Phoenix, Arizona, to small towns in North Carolina, Texas, and Wisconsin, from seven years in Washington, DC, to five years in Asia. Born and raised a small-town kid, he's as comfortable in Tokyo or Tuna, Texas. The variety of places he's lived serve as settings for the characters who invade his head.

He has four novels published with Evolved Publishing – *Slade*, *Turning Trixie*, *Hannah's Voice*, and *Carry Me Away*. His novels are best classified as contemporary southern lit. In 2022, Evolved also launched *June Bug Gothic: Tales from the South*, a collection of Robb's short stories.

Robb is also a sought-after fiction editor, with editing clients from around the world, including agented, traditionally published, and best-selling independent authors. His articles on the craft of writing fiction have appeared in various writer magazines and websites. He also has taught writing courses for the Romance Writers of America (even though he's not a romance writer), Romance Writers of Australia (even though he's not Australian), and is an instructor at the Novel-in-Progress Book Camp.

Robb now resides in the Ozarks of Missouri, where he writes and edits full time.

Website: https://www.robbgrindstaff.com
https://robbgrindstaff.substack.com
Facebook: https://www.facebook.com/robbgrindstaffwriter/
Twitter: https://twitter.com/RobbWriter

Keys to Finding an Agent or Publisher

Sarah Bullen

"I wasn't going to give up until every single publisher turned me down, but I often feared that would happen."
~ J.K. Rowling

As a literary agent with 17 years of working with authors, I read a lot of manuscripts (MS), and I get a lot of query letters. It always amazes me the huge effort and investment it takes to simply write a full-length book. When I get a MS in my inbox, I know this is a minimum of a year of somebody's life in my hands. More often it is actually a decade of work that has gone into the dreaming and then the writing of just one book.

Sadly, very often I wish the author had known some more of the basics of how the publishing industry worked before they invested so much time in a manuscript.

It really helps to understand exactly how books are secured for publication, sold, what your genre is, who your reader is, and what is required to get the book over its final few thresholds and into a printed product. If an author knows these things, agents can see it immediately. Even the query letter will spark attention. It will make me open more, perhaps the book synopsis.

Now if that is slick and interesting, I will look at the first three chapters. These are the steps any agent or publisher will take. So that means as an author you have to work these documents very hard and carefully to make sure they land well.

But let's take a step back and look at what you (as the author) need to get in place in order to actually attach documents and press SEND.

And yes, sending off a manuscript is terrifying. It is adrenaline-inducing, heart-stopping stuff for any writer.

So many writers bail or fail at this critical point. They send their book off to three agents or publishers and get one rejection letter. Then they put that MS in a bottom drawer and don't send it again.

This is not called submitting a book. Submitting a book is a long process that requires work and persistence. Give yourself a year.

Remember, this is ultimately a sales game. Few writers send their proposals to one agent or publisher and magically get picked up by the first one. Yes, it can and does occasionally happen. If you are crystal clear on your genre, have a knockout proposal, know the current publishing climate, your book is highly contemporary/timeless/a great story or you have *a big platform and author brand*, then maybe the first publisher you approach will sign you up. But in my experience, that is HIGHLY unlikely.

As an agent, it can take me *up to a year* to get a book publishing deal for an author. It is a combination of so many elements that come together to make a publisher say YES. To be honest, most of it is luck, contacts, good timing, and simply having a good book to show them.

The truth is that this 'being an author' is a long game, and along the journey you have to keep the momentum up, process any rejection letters, implement any feedback, get back to it, and keep going. Rinse and repeat. Rinse and repeat.

The purpose of this chapter is to help you to pull together some key tight pieces of writing to support your query and a ready-to-go "Pitch Deck" that will capture the attention of the agent or publisher you seek.

A Pitch Deck is a term borrowed from movies for all the documents you will gather together for that final step—pitching your book. There are a few elements to this, depending on your genre.

In a novel, you will need your full novel synopsis (the entire plot of your book in a tight 3-5 pages), an exciting covering (query) letter, and your first few chapters.

In a non-fiction book, your Pitch Deck includes your query letter, your full book proposal of 2-5 pages, and your first 3-5 chapters.

This chapter does not cover how to write your novel synopsis/proposal, but rather how to take these documents and bring them all together into the final form which you will send off. If you are in any doubt about how to write these key documents, please spend some time on that in order to get the format correct.

The assumption in this chapter is that you know what these two key documents are and have written them again and again until they are word perfect.

Here's what I've discovered leads to the most successful pitches.

Consider a Beta Reader or Professional Appraisal

I *highly recommend* that writers have a full manuscript critique before thinking 'I am ready, this is my final draft'. Don't waste years trying to sell and promote a book that simply really isn't ready for publication. In fact, many books I get feel more like a first draft. You may need to fix or improve it one last time.

A beta reader is a peer who will read your book and give you an honest report. It is important this person does not know you and that you find them through a group or a reference. A friend will just flatter you.

A far better bet is to get a professional editor to assess it. A manuscript appraisal is a commercial assessment that gives you a fresh, objective outsider's perspective and is done by a qualified editor. The overall aim of this high-level assessment is to improve your MS and give you real ways to make it better and more publishable. During the process, they will make significant notes and suggest changes. At the end of the process, you will get a full written report. The report will be an assessment of the manuscript, but it will also make suggestions and changes.

Some editors will also make detailed edit notes on your manuscript, or comments, for you.

The bonus here is that you can also use the comments as "endorsements" on your pitch documents or as a cover blurb or logline (if they are flattering).

Create Killer Back Cover Copy

Writing these tight pieces can be even tougher than writing your entire manuscript. Or it certainly feels that way. The reason is that it is often done after the fact when you just want the book over and done.

But there's no escape—to send off your book you MUST write these things. A good blurb most often sells your book. This is also a piece of writing that will work hard. Most often you will send this in the body of an email to a publisher or agent as your query letter and put it into your book proposal or synopsis. The back-cover copy functions as the primary advert for your book and will form the basis of your AI–Advance Information Sheet–the document publishers will send out to the bookstores and to the media.

Once your book is on sale, the back cover blurb is the thing after your title and front cover image that readers look at when deciding whether to make a purchase.

This blurb needs to sell your book and make it sound exciting and engaging. At this stage, it has to sell an agent or publisher.

It will be one or two tight paragraphs that should identify the essence of your story.

In non-fiction, this should be a short statement. Aim for 250-500 words maximum. Make a clear statement of what the book is about and why it is important.

In a novel, this tight piece of writing needs to be SO crafted and SO clever. It captures your main idea or question, your main character, the conflict they're going to face, and the stakes if they lose.

It also needs to make your book seem dramatic and desperately exciting (far more than it possibly really is).

I have a great formula for novels that you are welcome to use. Here it is:

Novel Back Cover Blurb Cheat Sheet

1. Introduce your main character

I like to see a razor-sharp three-word descriptor:

> Hollywood homicide detective Petra Connor (Johnathan Kellerman, *Twisted*)

Beautiful and brilliant Polish agent Liliana Pilecki (Tom Clancy)

2. What starts the adventure?

This inciting incident needs to set up your entire story, and it is the critical kick-start to your book. Reveal the inciting incident here in an incredibly exciting way that weaves in the character journey:

> When he receives a worrying phone call from his ex-wife (James Patterson)
> A body is discovered in an empty Atlanta warehouse (Karin Slaughter)

3. Hint at the plot of the book

We need to know what is going to happen. This is a balance between revealing too much and not revealing enough. In a way, *the entire blurb* is hinting at the plot (whereas your synopsis is fully revealing the entire plot):

> Rory's only choice is to find the killer himself. He risks his job, his pride, and his reputation to pursue the truth. (James Patterson)
> They begin to unravel a dark and appalling family history. (Stieg Larsson)

4. Tag only the other most important character (and keep the others nameless)

We want the reader to meet the biggest other player—but max two. Keep to the three-word rule here with a tight description. Anyone else gets a common noun e.g. 'mentor':

When Langdon's mentor—a prominent mason and phil-
anthropist—is kidnapped ... (Dan Brown)
(Connie) sails with her husband and son and the enig-
matic boat dealer
Bosch is partnered with fiery rookie detective Lucia Soto
(Michael Connelly)
A notorious Washington power broker (John Grisham)

5. Locate the reader in the story world and setting

This is where you drop some hard-working facts into your book.
Make sure your readers know in which era or location your book
is set. This may be as specific as listing a city or year, or more
general:

Set in Malaya 1941 (Kate Furnivall)
Secretive clan (Stieg Larsson)

6. Throw in some genre-specific words

Cold case murder investigation (Ian Rankin)
A powerful spell (Jeanine Frost)
As the body count rises (David Baldacci)
An ancient world of hidden wisdom . . . shadowy mythic
world (Dan Brown)

7. Crank up the drama

Use big words. Make this seem like the biggest deal in the world.
Nobody wants to read an average story. Yawn.

Ballard knows it is always darkest before dawn. But what
she doesn't know—yet—is how deep her investigation
will take her into the dark heart of her city, the police
department, and her own past . . . (Michael Connelly)

And standing up for the truth means putting your life on the line . . . (John Grisham)

Example - Fiction

The Hunger Games by Suzanne Collins:

> Panem, a shining Capitol surrounded by twelve outlying districts. The Capitol is harsh and cruel and keeps the districts in line by forcing them all to send one boy and one girl between the ages of twelve and eighteen to participate in the annual Hunger Games, a fight to the death on live TV. Sixteen-year-old Katniss Everdeen regards it as a death sentence when she steps forward to take her sister's place in the Games. But Katniss has been close to dead before, and survival, for her, is second nature. Without really meaning to, she becomes a contender. But if she is to win, she will have to start making choices that weigh survival against humanity and life against love.

Get a Cracking Author Blurb

An author blurb is another key element of all pitches that you need to work and rework. It will form part of your book proposal/synopsis—the final document you are going to send to agents and publishers if you want to present your book idea to them.

Writing a good one that sums up your personality, qualifications, and book in a few succinct words is so unbelievably useful for so many reasons. Nobody writes these but you!

- It will end up on the cover or inside cover of your book.
- It will be used in all marketing communications for publicity for your book.
- You can use it on your blog/website/CV.

- You can submit it to Wikipedia/LinkedIn as your page profile.
- You will use it on your Amazon/GoodReads author page.

General Format to use:

- Sentence 1: Include your name and surname along with two tight adjectives—this is your core identity or qualities. Write in 3rd person.
- Sentence 2 - 4: How have you lived this story? Give a short list as to what is going to support this story.
- Sentence 5: What is this going to reveal in the book?

Example - Non-Fiction (Inspirational)

Resilience from the Heart by Gregg Braden

Scientist Gregg Braden realized early in his career that neither science nor spirituality could provide a complete picture of how to live the best life. He has travelled the world for over 30 years visiting some of the most pristine, undisturbed and remote places around the globe in an effort to glean the wisdom of our ancestors so he could combine it with cutting-edge science. The result of what he learned is found in this book. *Resilience from the Heart* is written with you in mind. Within these pages, you'll find everything you need to embrace the biggest challenges in life and do so in a healthy way.

Example - Memoir (Celebrity)

Extreme by Sharon Osborne

Sharon Osborne was born in London in 1952. She is married to rock legend Ozzy Osbourne and has three children.

Craft a Powerful Logline

More tight writing. Oh yes.

This piece of writing is even shorter, tighter, and presents the book's main concept. In a novel, the logline captures your main idea or question/your main character/the conflict they're going to face/the stakes if they lose. We're talking short and high-level concept. It is one sentence, and this sentence utilises puns or clever wording to intrigue the reader. It should make them want to read the book or learn more. It often teases the reader or poses a question to them.

It's the line you will rest on when someone corners you next time with the dreaded question: 'What's your book about?'

Some people claim that loglines should be less than twenty-five words long. I don't think publishers and agents sit there counting the number of words in your logline, I think they want to understand the core story. Imagine your book in a catalogue of many; this is the one line you have to tell readers what it is.

Do not use names. Include the book title.

There is no formula. Just make your best effort for now.

Examples - Non-Fiction

Fall Out: A Memoir of Friends Made and Friends Unmade by Jane Street-Porter
Friends. Everyone needs them. Especially when relations between you and your family are less than perfect.
Find Your Extraordinary by Jessica Herrin shows that you don't need to have it all to live an extraordinary life—you need to have what matters most to you.

Examples - Novels

The Firm by John Grisham
When a Harvard Law School grad joins a prestigious
firm, he ignores the warning of his wife, who fears the
lucrative deal may be too good to be true.
Harry Potter and the Sorcerer's Stone by J.K. Rowling
A boy wizard begins training and must battle for his life
with the Dark Lord who murdered his parents.

Reference Bigger Names

Another element that makes a huge difference in your pitch is
putting in some key markers about what style the book is
written in. Pop this right up front in the query letter.

Yes, I see you have written a New Adult novel, but give me
something to link it to. Here I like to see some big literary
names in the genre that I (or anyone else) would know.

Use at least two to really locate your book style in the mind of
the agent. You can reference a movie or television show as well,
but make sure to segment yourself with an author, too. I would
actually include this as a full sentence in the query letter or just
after your logline:

> e.g. This is a John Grisham-style legal thriller set in the
> world of cryptocurrency with the darker style of Ozark.

> This book is a sassy tell-all memoir like *Air Babylon* or
> *Confessions of an Expat in Paris* set in the world of polo
> pony breeding.

Hone Your Search

It is critical to only send your book to a publisher or agent who
works in your genre. Sounds simple? Not so. This is going to
take work and lots of it.

If you send your book on *'101 Uses for an Airfryer'* to an agent/publisher who publishes Young Adult Fiction it is an instant fail.

Here you need to be specific and focused. Get to the nitty gritty, not just CRIME, but do they particularly like your kind of crime story (and I mean here your sub-genre—a forensic detective story vs. female sleuth vs. amateur detective)?

Take a trip to the bookshop. Find your genre, look on your own bookshelf, and browse The Writers Marketplace or Amazon.com to research publishing houses that fall on your dream publishing list. Make sure you also browse the internet to research all the agents and publishing houses that might be a good fit.

Note down the relevant publishers and agents. Choose most of your hit list from your home.

Is your book in English? Then look at all the English-speaking countries as a first stop: UK, Ireland, Canada, USA, Australia, New Zealand, and South Africa.

Join online writing groups to network, connect, and get ideas. Check Twitter for some hot new agents looking for new authors. Chat with any authors you know for leads and ideas. Follow relevant publishers on social media to stay up-to-date with their submission windows and publishing guidelines.

Then refine your search to the particular commissioning editor or agent who handles your specific genre.

Pull it Together in a Sizzling Author Query Letter

You have done all the work—written your logline, back cover blurb, and author bio, and crafted your book proposal. You have written it again and again until it is darn near perfect. It sings. You now have your entire pitch deck ready.

Now what? How does this all come together?

You are going to send all these documents off to an agent/publisher with a simple query letter, which is basically a well-crafted email.

It is the very first thing (and often the only thing) an agent or publisher is going to see. In the old days, this used to be posted as a typed single sheet of paper. But now we email query letters or submit them online.

Ideally, when the agent or publisher opens the submission, they will see the main idea of your book in a few lines.

As noted above, the query letter should compel the reader to open the other documents attached . . . which is your knockout book proposal and first few chapters.

You will write one of these and then paste it into each letter you send to a publisher or agent. Tailor each one with their name and a personalization.

You will also copy and paste this into online submission platforms such as 'Submittable.'

Part One—Get your genre clear

State the title and genre in the subject line and again in the body of the email.

Part Two—About your book

Go straight in and give them your best blurb. Grab the one from your book proposal. It should be around two to three short paragraphs. If you can't get it down . . . work on it. The agent will decide if they want more of your book based on this basic summary, so do make sure you send your very best version.

Part Three—About you

This is a short background that cues them into who you are. This is shorter than the full one in your proposal so get it down to around 2-3 sentences. Set yourself up as qualified to write this book. What is it that you do—are you a life coach, surgeon, pro athlete, dog lover, property broker? For a memoir, you need to highlight important things about yourself and your life.

Part Four—Close it up

Phew! Almost done! Sign off. And that's all there is to it.

Hit Send

This is where the rubber hits the road. So many writers stumble at this unavoidable key step. The dreaded submission process. This is NOT the time to be shy or hold back.

Do you believe in this book? Did you invest your time in it?

Now change gears from a writer into a salesperson and get this book SOLD!

You are going to send at least TWENTY query letters on your first shot.

Yes, that's right. At least 20. This is not a loyalty game—you are trying to find one agent or publisher that actually reads the MS so you need to be bold. Think of it like Tinder, the popular dating app. You have to swipe right a lot to make a match.

Any salesperson will tell you that sales are a numbers game. The more people you contact, the better chance you have of a sale.

You should send your book out to as many publishers and agents as possible. And then you need to keep sending it out. Now, this is not as easy as it seems.

You are selling your book so start working the numbers!

There are some key beats you cannot miss when you hit send.

Be flexible. Some publishers will ask you to submit online and will allow only specific word counts for each section. Take your best versions and fit them into their formats.

- Check their requirements first. Some don't want your first three chapters. Some want 10,000 words. Check if they want Word documents or PDFs. Many use Submittable or an online form that has a fixed word count.

- Check if they have a naming protocol and follow it. Name your documents in a logical and consistent way. Usually, this is BOOK TITLE_synopsis and BOOK TITLE_Chapters.

- Have all your documents properly formatted (read their requirements on font size and spacing) and add a footer on all documents that have this information: BOOK TITLE + AUTHOR NAME + DATE + PAGE NUMBER.

No matter how many books you have written, this is always the moment you have your heart right up there in your throat. J.K. Rowling must have felt this again when she submitted her crime novel *The Cuckoo's Calling* under the pseudonym Robert Galbraith. Rowling also sent her novel out to an estimated dozen publishers. Kate Mills, publishing director of Orion, was one of the publishers who rejected it.

> "When the book came in, I thought it was perfectly good," she was quoted widely as saying. "It was certainly well written —but it didn't stand out." Ouch.

The novel was rejected by an estimated dozen publishers.

Be Annoyingly Persistent

Allocate a year to keep sending. Gasp! So long?

I need to be persistent as an agent. It can take me a year to sell a book. You need to be equally so as a writer. I have recently spent close to 12 months following up on a single manuscript sent to a publisher who finally commissioned it.

But the commissioning agent was 'very busy' and just didn't get to it. No reply. Then she went on holiday. Then maternity leave. For every email I sent to follow up, only about one out of five were returned. I am the agent in this transaction so it is my job to keep going. But let me tell you that if I were the book's writer, I would have taken it very personally and given up or just thought they had dropped me. In fact, it turns out that the publishing company does want the book, they just moved that particular imprint out a year, and we got lost in the day-to-day of running a big imprint.

So don't give up. If the book is 'in play', you need to keep playing. You will know it is no longer in play when they tell you. It will be something like this . . . "Thank you for your submission, but we will not be publishing your book. / Thank you, but this book is not for us, best of luck."

That's a no. Now move on to the next mailshot of 20. Anything else is a maybe.

Author and motivational speaker Jack Canfield talks about how he approached 144 publishers with his little book *Chicken Soup for the Soul.* After 14 months, he and co-author Mark Victor Hanson almost gave up. Finally, the 145th decided to take a chance on them—the result is a billion-dollar empire that is now a household name and has sold 500 million books. Imagine if they gave up after the first, 10^{th,} or 144th?

Keep the Faith

Writing any book takes a huge commitment of your time, faith, and yourself. Of course, it is wonderful to find an agent, and they do all this for you, but agents are rare, and you may have to submit everything yourself. I also know that it is very hard to promote yourself. If you do feel you cannot find the courage— then find a friend or hire someone who can do it for you. But the best submissions come from the writers themselves.

Always remember that publishers are in the business of looking for exciting new books.

If you want to be successful, and a published author, you need to have three things. You need a completed book, you need buckets of courage, and you need some luck.

It was not brilliant writing which made E.L. James' *50 Shades of Gray* a massive hit. It was the decision to self-publish digitally and then through The Writers Coffee Shop that first got it out there. And then reader reviews and EL James' strong online presence (along with book blogs) took it global. There is no single way to get a book into the world. Explore all your options.

You have done the work. Send it out and leave some of it to fate.

What Makes a Book Successful?

It is not as complicated as it seems, but it requires a few things.

- An author with commitment and a good idea
- A polished, professional, and *completed* book
- A well-crafted book proposal or synopsis
- A manuscript as close to perfect as you can make it
- A great cover and title
- A publisher and a publishing deal
- The best possible editor
- Being published at the right time
- Strong reviews
- Luck

Top 10 Countdown to Successfully Finding an Agent or Publisher

10. Utilize beta readers or content appraisers to improve your finished copy.

9. Create killer back cover copy.

8. Get a crackling author bio.

7. Craft a powerful logline.

6. Reference bigger names.

5. Hone your search for agents and publishers.

4. Pull it together in a sizzling query letter.

3. Hit send.

2. Be annoyingly persistent.

1. Keep the faith.

Meet Sarah Bullen

Sarah Bullen is a multi-published author, international writing coach and literary agent. Founder of The Writing Room www.thewritingroom.co.za and Kent Literary Agency. She has had over 130 books published by writers she has mentored. As well as being a regular guest on the craft of writing on talk shows, podcasts and writers' circles, Sarah has been leading international writing retreats and adventures for the past decade.

Her recent books include *Write your Book in 100 Days! Stop Mucking About and Just Write It* and *Love and Above: A Journey through Shamanism, Coma and Joy.*

Facebook: @sarahbullenwritingroom

Instagram: thewritingroom.sarahbullen

The Transformational Path to Publishing Success

Christine Kloser

It was October of 2002 and I had been dreaming about becoming an author for more than a decade. Since the early '90s, I had collected bits and pieces of writing here and there for a book I would have titled *Rules From the Road.*

The premise was that the signs and signals we see on the road, and in our own cars, had valuable messages for us about life. At the time, I was a personal fitness trainer in Los Angeles who drove all over the city to get to clients' homes for sessions. I saw a lot of road signs, experienced a lot of cars, freeways, traffic jams, and aggressive drivers. I learned a lot from the many hours a week I spent behind the wheel.

Yet, through all those years, my book never got published because I had no idea how to transform words in a document on my computer into a printed, published book. Back then, print on demand wasn't widely available, and the Kindle hadn't even been invented yet. It'd be five more years before anyone read a book on a Kindle device. My book went nowhere.

So, when my husband had an inspired idea for a book in October of 2002, I was shocked to hear myself tell him that if he figured out how to write it, I'd figure out how to publish it. You see, he wanted to interview Major League Baseball players to write a book for young athletes that helped them understand the importance of mindset/mental game to help them succeed in a game where the best players fail more than 70% of the time.

It was a wonderful ambition; however, he didn't know any Major League Baseball players, nor did he know anyone who did. The chances of him getting all these interviews were slim to none from my perspective.

Flash forward two years and he figured out how to get more than 300 interviews with top players from all thirty Major League Baseball teams, as well as Hall of Fame players and team managers. It was an incredible journey for him to hang out on the field during warm-ups, spend time with the players in the clubhouse, and watch games from the press box. He was in his glory! I was standing by wondering what the heck I got myself into.

Now I had to hold up my end of the bargain and figure out how to publish a book. Thankfully, I'm a very resourceful woman, and I figured it out. I learned so much about publishing that in addition to publishing my husband's book in 2004, I also published my first book, which was a collection of stories written by myself and thirty-nine women entrepreneur colleagues.

That book was titled *Inspiration to Realization,* and I was thrilled to finally become an author. I felt both excitement and relief to check "become a published author" off my bucket list. I thought that would be the beginning and end of my journey as an author and publisher.

Little did I know that was only the start of my journey as an author, coach, and publisher who has since helped more than 600 people fulfill their dream of getting published. Many of our clients have become best-sellers and award-winners, have been invited to speak at TEDx, grew significant six- and seven-figure business, and appeared nationwide on major media outlets. In total, more than 80,000 aspiring authors have been impacted by my live events, virtual trainings, and online programs. I never could have imagined all this would happen from my husband's idea for his book, *Stepping Up to the Plate.*

But the road to get from that first book to here hasn't been a straight one, nor an easy one. The transformational path to my publishing success has been filled with twists, turns, highs, and lows. But what I have learned along the way has proven to be life-changing for the *Get Your Book Done* program members and Capucia publishing clients we serve.

Following, I'll share some details about my journey and teach you the four critical steps to take on your transformational path to publishing success.

But first, how I came to know what I know today, which is the only true way to write and publish a book that changes lives is to take it on as a transformational process. You must appreciate that writing your book will change your life *first*, and then deeply impact and transform the lives of your readers.

I learned this truth the hard way. It started two years after my first anthology, *Inspiration to Realization,* was published. I had believed I was a one-and-done author. But with the help of a great publicist, my very first was featured on the pages of the print edition of *Entrepreneur* magazine as one of the "best books" for women entrepreneurs to read in the Summer of 2005.

This accomplishment and recognition was huge for me, and all of the women who contributed to the book, especially as a first-time self-published author. This kind of publicity didn't usually happen for books like mine. But this time it did, and I was thrilled.

After word spread through my community of women entrepreneurs, those who had missed out on contributing to my first book were now begging me to let them know when I'd be compiling Volume 2. Wait, what? I had no intention of putting together a Volume 2! But they were persistent, and I'm a softie when it comes to helping people fulfill a dream. So, I put together Volume 2 and Volume 3 of that series and have since published more than sixteen anthology books featuring authors from nearly twenty countries.

But here's the thing that happened that helped me get to where I am today and what I most want you to learn from my experience. The women in my first few anthologies gained incredible confidence, clarity, and courage in working with me to see their wisdom, experience, story, and knowledge on the pages of a published book. So much so that they quickly began asking me to help them write their own book.

This was another one of those, "Wait, what?" type of moments. Of course, I couldn't help them do that, as I had never written my own book. I, too, had only written a chapter in one of my books up to that point. Their requests went on for more than a year, and I could tell they weren't going to let up. And in one divinely-orchestrated moment, two of those women came to me separately but simultaneously and said, "You have to help me write my book!" What happened next was me hearing myself say, "Yes, I will" before my brain could stop the words from coming out of my mouth.

All I could think was "Oh, crumb! Now I have to write my own book, and I have no idea how to do that." I'm not the kind of person who will teach anyone anything I haven't yet done myself. I literally had to figure out how to write my own book so I could show them how to write theirs. I planned a day for myself at the Chocolate Spa at the Hotel Hershey so I could get away from my everyday environment and figure out how to write a book.

It was a magical day of insight, research, intuition, and creation. Thank goodness, because I had already enrolled six people into my yet-to-be-named program, and I was starting with them in a few weeks. So, there, sitting poolside at the hotel, I received the name of the program, *Get Your Book Done*®, secured the domain www.getyourbookdone.com that very day, and put together enough structure on how to write a book that I felt confident I could deliver a great program.

Before our first group session, I put myself through my own paces and started laying out the structure for my first solo book, *The Freedom Formula: How to Put Soul in Your Business and Money In Your Bank.* I facilitated my *Get Your Book Done* coaching group twice a month, went through exercises, work-sheets, and manuscripts, and had a productive six months of coaching everyone to write their books at the same time I wrote my own. They were all successfully published by my company and went on to do amazing things as a result of the clout and credibility that authorship brings.

For me, though, the journey was different. It was 2008, and I was nearing the end of publishing my book. I remember feeling like something was "off." I have a clear vision of being in Las Vegas at a mastermind with my then coach. I stood at the front of the room, unable to hold the tears back from streaming down my face. All I could say was, "I know it all looks great on the outside, but it doesn't feel right on the inside." I had an event lined up based on my book in a few months, and tickets were already sold. I was able to get *New York Times* best-selling author Neale Donald Walsch to write the foreword for my book. I had lots of strong endorsements from industry experts. Yet, inside of myself, none of it felt right.

At that time, *The Freedom Formula* felt like a book I was supposed to read, not yet a book I was qualified to write. I was grateful to be there at the mastermind with my coach, husband, and colleagues to navigate these murky waters, with the book being well underway, but not feeling right in my soul. But the coach and all my colleagues pretty much disregarded what I was feeling and told me that it was just my fear kicking in because everything I dreamed of was starting to happen. I just needed to keep going and not let fear stop me.

I wasn't then who I am now, and I took their advice and followed it to a "T." I did everything "right," sold a few thousands books when we launched, and got more than one hundred people to attend my *Freedom Formula Experience* in January, 2009. At that event, I was successful in enrolling more than twenty people into my 12-month *Freedom Formula Mastermind.* Everything looked perfect on the outside.

Inside I was a wreck. The whole thing felt out of alignment with who I was and the work I was here to do. Certainly I was, and am, here to help people learn how to put soul in their businesses, their books, and their lives. But what it seemed everyone wanted from me was the "put money in your bank" part of my process . . . without the other part that was the core of who I am.

This made for a very challenging year, and the unthinkable, but personally necessary, decision to pull the plug on everything I was doing after my clients graduated the program. My coach, mentors, and colleagues all said I was crazy and should just keep going because nobody had the kind of success I experienced right out of the gate with a new book and program. My event planner was, perhaps, the most shocked when I told her I wouldn't be renewing my contract with the hotel to host my *Freedom Formula Experience* event again.

I simply couldn't do it. Every cell of my being knew that book and that message—while helpful to thousands of people, even now more than a decade later—was not what I was meant to be doing as my life's work.

With my husband's support, we rode the rough waters of shutting everything down so I could figure out how exactly I was meant to help people. Because it certainly wasn't as one more "guru" telling people how to make money. That wasn't what I was here for. That rough road led to a devastating bankruptcy and losing our home to foreclosure. These were some of the darkest days of my life, while also being the most transformational.

Amidst the experience of losing everything around me of material value, I went inward. I spent hours a day in silence. Meditating, journaling, praying, asking and begging the Universe to show me the purpose of the pain. There were days I thought I'd be better off crawling under a rock for the rest of my life, hiding from everyone due to the shame and embarrassment of what I was going through. Thankfully, there were more days than not when I could feel a spark of hope, a new possibility that something profound and powerful was happening there in the murkiness of my struggle.

In a flash of a moment during the pre-dawn hours one day while I was meditating in early 2011, the clarity about what was next came to me. I was meant to figure out a way to merge the work I'd done as a transformational facilitator (which I'd been doing since 1997 when I started leading women's retreats as a side-gig in the mountains of Lake Arrowhead, California), with the work I'd been doing serving authors since 2002 (when I started supporting my husband on his author journey).

Yes! Everything about this felt right in my cells. I could stand in integrity—inside of bankruptcy and foreclosure—and teach this! I knew it with every ounce of my being that this is what I was meant to do. So, I picked myself up and got to work. I decided I would host a virtual summit I had considered holding the year prior, named the *Transformational Author Experience*. But I never did this in 2010 because a lot of my colleagues told me it was a terrible name and would never work. That nobody would attend an event called that.

But there, in February, 2011, I knew this was literally the *only* thing I could do to be true to myself, while regaining financial stability for my family, and serving aspiring authors with this new approach to becoming an author.

The only challenge was that when I went to Google to search "transformational author," it was crickets. Nothing showed up. There was no prior mention of those two words together on the Internet. Which meant this concept was brand new, but it also meant I had to figure out what a transformational author was.

I knew how difficult it was to have the wrong book lead to a misaligned business and lose everything as a result. I also knew experiencing this was the perfect preparation for this new approach. I never wanted anyone to experience what I had gone through. So, this new journey was about me learning how to write (and teach other aspiring authors how to write) a book that was truly the right book for the author. A book that felt like the perfect expression of who they are in the world, the wisdom they're here to share. One that aligned with every cell of their being. The book they were born to write.

That is what it means to be a transformational author. This is how my team and I have been blessed to witness hundreds of lives transform as we guide would-be authors from book "idea" to published author. This is all possible because of a tool I created and wrote a book about called *The Transformation Quadrant®*. It was a tool I didn't have when I wrote *The Freedom Formula*, but is one I wish for every author to use so they can learn from my struggle.

This tool provides the four foundational steps every author needs to take before writing a word of their book. It helps make sure you don't end up like I did, writing a book that isn't the right one. My wish is that in sharing this tool with you, you will experience a much more joyful and easy transformational path to publishing success.

The Transformation Quadrant consists of four essential questions. Questions I didn't know were necessary when I created the first iteration of my *Get Your Book Done* program and wrote my first book. Questions that tens of thousands of authors have since been taught, and it changed the trajectory of their books in beautiful ways they never knew possible.

The first question of *The Transformation Quadrant* is, "What transformation do you want for your SELF as you write your book?" Writing a life-changing book begins with you as the author and it's essential you approach the writing of your book as the transformational process it is. That journey begins when you answer this question and dig a little deeper to uncover the truth about yourself and how you want writing this book to change things for the better. You may want to gain more confidence, let go of self-doubt, step into your power more fully, embody your expertise in a deeper way, etc. There is no wrong answer here.

The second question of *The Transformation Quadrant* is, "What transformation do you want for your READER as they read your book?" Imagine your ideal reader holding your book in their hands after reading the very last page. What transformation, hope, new possibility do you want for them now that they've received the wisdom, information, stories in your book? This question helps you connect more deeply with your reader, which helps you write more powerfully for them and connect with them through your words.

The third question of *The Transformation Quadrant* is, "What transformation do you want for your BUSINESS as a result of your book being in the world." Your book is like a key that can turn on the engine of your business in a powerful way. It's essential to get clear on how you want your book to transform your business. Do you want it to get your phone ringing with new client inquiries, leverage it to gain media attention, establish expertise and open new doors of opportunity? Get a literary agent? Become a best-seller? Turn your book idea into a movie? You must know the connection between your book and your business in order to ensure you're writing the right book and growing the right business.

All authors, even those of you writing fiction, must consider the business outcomes you expect in writing and publishing your book. You have already invested time and energy and will continue to do so through the publishing and marketing elements of getting your book out into the world. Agented or not, self-published or not, answering this Quadrant business question is essential to your definition of success. Take it from one who knows what it's like to not do this from the start.

And the final question of *The Transformation Quadrant* is, "What transformation do you want for the WORLD as a result of your book?" When you look at the larger impact your book can have —whether that is millions of people across the globe, or the "world" in your own town or city—imagine what can change in the world when people read your book, get the transformation and live their life differently as a result of what they learned from you. Amazing to think about, isn't it!

I highly encourage you to take some time to do *The Transformation Quadrant,* preferably before the end of the day today, so it's fresh in your mind. The transformational path to publishing success begins with this. It begins with you writing the right book, for the right reasons, and feeling deeply connected to the transformations you desire on all four of these levels.

Beyond that, your publishing success depends on finding the right publishing path for your book. Once you've got the right book, it's essential you consider things like:

- The value you place on high quality standards for editing, design, and production.
- Building a big enough author platform to get the attention of a traditional publisher.
- Where you stand on maintaining rights to your book, or selling those rights for an advance.
- The amount of time you're willing to wait to see your book published.
- How much you're willing to learn and figure out on your own versus hiring experts to help you.

These few questions will help you determine if working with a traditional, hybrid or independent publisher is best for you, or if you'd be better off self-publishing.

The good news about publishing a book today is there are no longer any barriers to keep you from publishing successfully. You can do this! Write the right book, assess your publishing options and choose the one that's right for you. Then, watch as your book comes to life and readers are impacted by your message. Happy writing!

Top 10 Countdown to Publishing

10. Do *The Transformation Quadrant*.

9. Get support to write your best book.

8. Do not edit while you write, let the ideas flow.

7. Stay committed until the very last word.

6. Trust the process.

5. Explore the four publishing paths (traditional, self, hybrid, Indy).

4. Be realistic about which path is right for you.

3. Figure out the timeline for the path you chose and set your release date.

2. Start working on your marketing plans at least six months before your book is published.

1. Celebrate when your book launches, and never stop marketing.

Meet Christine Kloser

USA Today and *Wall Street Journal* best-selling author, Christine Kloser, is the Founder and CEO of Get Your Book Done and Capucia Publishing. With 650+ published author to date, her clients have leveraged their books to launch careers, grow six and seven-figure businesses, appear on TEDx and become sought after media experts in major outlets worldwide.

Authentic Voices

Natalie Obando

How Communities that are Typically Marginalized in Publishing Can Overcome the Systemic Challenges Embedded in the Book and Publishing World and What Non-Marginalized People Can Do to be Allies in Creating Equity

Publishing is an entirely new beast from the days I began my starry-eyed journey into a career I knew almost nothing about. What was taught at my West Coast university and what I came to experience from a predominantly East Coast-dominated field were quite different to say the very least. Nearly two decades ago, I was fresh out of college and excited, albeit naïve, about what the world of publishing had in store for my energetic mind, filled with ideas and stories that I was sure would solve the world's problems.

I've always been somewhat of an idealist and optimist. I credit that mentality to growing up poor, with a single mom and a father who, when I was six months old, was incarcerated for 34 years. My mother, ever the hard worker and with little childcare, would grab a book from the library and make me sit in a corner while she worked her second job. "Be quiet and don't talk to anyone," she would say as she worked into her eleventh hour. "Practice reading." So I did. In those moments, her employers would remark how well-behaved I was or how smart I was, but really, I was shutting everyone out. I was immersed in a world that I had constructed in my mind from words on a page. It was magic, and I was hooked.

Growing up, I was absolutely certain I would be a writer. There was no doubt in my mind, and at that time, those dreams were fueled by an encouraging family praising my many journals filled with short story after short story, usually based on something happening within our block's radius. My mom said I would more likely end up the town gossip, la chismosa, because I always knew what was going on in our close-knit neighborhood. I could also recite her private phone conversations to my abuela word for word. But as the years went on and I learned what bills were, how money worked, and how there seemed to be a very short supply of it for my family and communities like mine, the more other people's dreams of what I would become weighed me down. By the time I began college, the family consensus was that I study something that had to do with business. That, to them, seemed to be what would actually make money and be worth the financial investment in my future. In my family, going to school to be a writer wasn't "a thing," especially if it's a school that you're paying for. "Como que, *writer?*" my abuela would say in her Spanglish. She, and many other members of my family, made it very clear that writers don't get paid to write. And that for some reason you had to already be famous or white and rich to make it as a writer. They were partially correct.

So, I listened because adults and family know everything, right? I majored in journalism but snuck in a minor in creative writing. After college, I settled on somewhat of a mesh of the three things I was good at—gossip, writing, and books—and I became a literary publicist.

Sometimes I look back at that time and daydream of what might have become of my writing ambition if my family had actually fostered my creativity as an adult as they did when I was a child. I know now that they were somewhat correct in their assumptions about publishing, and my writing dreams might have been even more crushed when I found that out on my own. They already knew what years of being a brown immigrant in America had taught them—the systems, no matter what type, were predominantly made for communities not like ours. They knew that this extended to publishing.

Publishing in the United States is inherently a white industry with systems in place that cater to stories of white, cis gendered, able-bodied men and women. Those stories are told more often than any other demographic in the U.S. And while there might have been some early tales about non-white people in books, more often than not, they were told by a white man or woman. The trouble with those stories, told from a white gaze, was that they only showcased the hardships non-white communities, used stereotypes, and completely omitted the stories of who we truly were. Our stories were used and told back to us in a way that didn't reflect who we were and what our communities truly were.

From the earliest of times there have been many beautiful stories written by and for white men and women. Stories filled with glitz and glamor, or love and escapism, or heroism. Compare that astronomical number to the miniscule number of stories told by Black, indigenous and other people of color, and it is no wonder that many of us from communities of color feel as if we don't belong in publishing and as if our stories don't matter. Often, even those miniscule numbers of stories about communities of color were written by a white man or woman and the story is mostly centered on the strife and hardships of communities that they do not understand. Stories filled with stereotypes have cycled their way into our lives through educational systems as required reading and left our communities in a perpetual loop of discovering ourselves through a viewpoint that is not our own. Because that is often what books do to and for us, they allow us to discover ourselves through stories and imagination. Through the words on the page we often find our own potential.

Finding a book centered on the heart of our communities rather than one that told a story of a stereotype was very rare not that long ago. Sandra Cisneros, Octavia Butler, and Julia Alvarez's works are embedded into my soul because those were the only books I knew that had people in them that looked or shared commonalities with me and my community. Years after discovering the works of those great authors, the very first fun "chick lit" type book I read featuring a full cast of Latina characters was *The Dirty Girls Social Club* by Alisa Valdes, and it blew my mind. All these Latina characters were like the women of *Sex and the City*, like the group from *Friends*, or the countless other white main characters that I got to know and love and tried to emulate growing up. The women in *The Dirty Girls Social Club* weren't immigrants crossing borders, they weren't drug kingpin's wives, they weren't housekeepers or nannies, they were just Latinas living a full and colorful life with problems that had nothing to do with the stereotypes that often hijack Latinx narratives. This one book allowed me to identify with characters and life situations I knew and understood. Up until that point, publishing had only printed stories about grief and despair amongst communities of color, and after reading so much of that, I subconsciously believed it.

As an idealist and optimist, I have always thought things had to get better, right? That tends to be my mind frame when going into anything. And luckily for my career in publishing I've stuck to that positive mentality. After nearly twenty years of working in publishing, I have seen the dial slightly turn in favor of representation of BIPOC (Black Indigenous People of Color) stories in publishing. I have started to see a peppering of representation of BIPOC workers in publishing (sitting in acquisitions, HR, editorial, publicity and marketing roles), the dial is turning. Albeit slowly.

So why is this important to you? Well, chances are that if you are reading this book, you are curious about, or are on your path to, writing and publishing. Perhaps you've already finished your book or novel and are taking a look at this book to see what needs to be refined. Or maybe you're just starting out and want to see what potentially lies ahead on your writing journey. In any case, it is helpful to know the state of the publishing industry and what to expect, especially if you are part of a BIPOC community and even if you are not. If you are a BIPOC writer there is a history of practices in publishing that you should be aware of. As an ally, there are many ways to use your privilege to create equity in publishing.

The simple fact of the matter is that, after multiple police killings in 2020 sparked a second Civil Rights movement, the publishing industry was forced to analyze its outdated and oppressive practices and structures. With threads of discussions on social media like #publishingpaidme, normal everyday folk were able to see that publishing was designed by, and really only worked for, those already in higher class tiers. These discussions led to numerous BIPOC authors finding out that their books had made less in advances than white counterparts even if the BIPOC writers were seasoned authors who had a history of selling copies and a great platform to sell from. First-time white authors with little to no platform and little to no experience were making more at the start of their entrance into publishing. Publishing discussions exposed readers to who was making decisions about acquisitions and what folx (folks) in publishing offices were making financially. Most often, it was very little, especially compared to the cost of living in New York. What was revealed was what many of us already knew, that in order to make a living as an author, you had to already have some sort of wealth or a second job. And in order to get a start working at a publishing office, you had to begin as an unpaid or minimally paid intern and not be able to afford rent nearby. This often puts the financial strain on parents which in the case of many people, and especially BIPOC communities, isn't always feasible. So once again, the broken system hires people in acquisitions who come from wealth and can only really connect with stories that reflect their living experiences and the stereotypes that they've come to believe as truth.

And while all this information may seem very dismal to a BIPOC writer, the idealist in me wants you to know that publishing is working to make changes. More importantly, the fighter in me wants you to know that those BIPOC writers and professionals already in publishing, like me, are breaking down doors and demanding change from the inside out. Change is definitely happening. BIPOC communities within publishing are growing and unifying. We are making changes happen. And with the amazing new capabilities of self-publishing and hybrid publishing, combined with social media platforms and other ways to have your voices heard, well, there are many ways to get your story to the masses. Publishers no longer have all the power. Gatekeepers are watching as more and more BIPOC stories are flying off shelves, causing change and demand, and being the catalyst for a new and inclusive era in publishing. Your story is needed, and now the choice is in your hands about how to deliver your story.

Battling Imposter Syndrome

Many of us have held onto fear-based belief systems embedded in us. These are subconscious ways of behaving passed from our own family members and that have encouraged us to feel safe by being unseen. Imposter syndrome often plagues us. And why wouldn't it? Our entire existence has been quieted because gatekeeping equals retaining power. But if you are here and reading this, I hope your fear is diminishing. If you are here and still reading, know that you need to be heard.

Often, those who are BIPOC are often bogged down with less flow and more stop, assess, and go. As a BIPOC person, we don't always have the privilege of living in a state of flow where creativity can flourish. We are constantly assessing the systems in place around us for the sake of survival. When in this state, creativity takes a back seat. This can create a blueprint for our creative lives. When people from marginalized communities have to worry more about survival, even if it's subconsciously, creativity can be stifled. When I say that BIPOC communities worry about survival more than others, what I mean is that subconsciously we know that systems are not built for our success, but for the success of white cisgender men and women. This knowledge influences our writing and our ability to trust our life experiences and innate power. We are so conditioned to look at ourselves through the white gaze, that we often believe it. But we are not a monolith. We are different people from different rich cultures and rich experiences that have made us who we are. Our stories are worthy of being told. You cannot be an imposter of your own creativity.

Do you believe your story matters? Do you believe that the story that you are working on right now can impact the life of just one person, even if it's your own? If you answered yes to either of those questions, then the world needs your story and only you can tell it. If you still aren't sure, I invite you to begin your writing process and see what unfurls. The most beautiful and intimate part about storytelling is that your lived experiences influence your writing and that makes it unique to you. Sure, you might write stories similar to (insert author name here), or your memoir might be comparable to (insert famous person here), but no two stories are the same because of who you are when you write your story. Likewise, storytelling changes who you become during your writing process, and who you are at the end of it all. The process of writing your stories is symbiotic in nature to your evolution. Writing is similar to metamorphosis in that through your story you become who you always needed yourself to be. Still you, but stronger for having the courage to expose your story to all. Embrace the writer within, and surrender the judgements.

Find or Build a Supportive Community that Understands and Supports Your Writing

When I minored in Creative Writing, my absolute LEAST favorite part of my creative writing classes were the group critique sessions. I loved to write about moments of my culture that were dear and sacred to me, but many people in the class did not understand those moments, especially when they were rife with Spanglish. I remember writing about a sacred healing that took place in my neighborhood on a sick child by a local curandero in my abuela's home. I was very young when it happened but the process of it all struck me in a way that made me appreciate ceremony, ritual, and faith at an early age. I received many compliments about that piece, including from my instructor. My classmates and instructor also gave me notes on how to make it better, and I valued their input. But there was one student who tore my story to shreds. He "just didn't understand it." And found the "Spanglish weird."

"What was the point?" he asked.

This came from a blond-haired, blue-eyed, non-Indian man in my class who later wrote a piece about the Indian Goddess Kali in a way that, I felt, demonized the religion. But he felt his story was fast-paced and action-packed and in that way it made sense to him. Because he wasn't willing and open to learn more about the people and culture that he wrote about, or the culture and ceremony I was writing about, his opinions felt more like criticisms of my culture and heritage rather than my writing.

Writing is such a heartfelt process. It unearths all that you are. And it is because of this that it's important for writers to find a community that supports them and their writing. I'm in no way suggesting you need a bunch of "yes" people around you during the writing process, but you do need people in your corner who understand or are willing to learn who you are and where you are writing from. It is because of this that I truly believe community is essential.

Those new to the art of writing often need guidance so that they don't get stuck in a rut and just throw their hands up in the air and give up on that project for weeks or months, or even worse, forever. When we do fall into a writing rut, and I can almost guarantee that you will at least once, we all do, it is wonderful to have people around you who are willing to coach you out of it. If you don't have that community, it is very easy to fall susceptible to the whispers of family or friends wondering what the heck you're doing and why the heck you're doing it. We writers are a different beast and we understand the need to release our stories and let them run wild until we can tame them. But those who aren't writers cannot possibly know that yearning for the liberation writing gives to you.

Community for BIPOC writers is especially important because our communities don't always have the resources needed when it comes to insight, connection, education, and proximity to publishing. An example of this might be our parents being immigrants without a secondary education or even language barriers. It could also be not having a creative writing program in your public schools because of lack of funding and having to start your writing from a place a little further back than others you know. It could be not knowing anything about the writing world because where you're from, there are no writers. It's intimidating. These types of resources are privileges that often come at the cost of exclusion of marginalized communities. These act as gatekeepers in publishing. However, coming together in solidarity helps to gather and construct some of those resources. In my work in building the Authentic Voices fellowship, I was able to pull resources together for the sake of bringing them to marginalized communities. I gathered the creative writing instructors I knew, the editors that I knew, and the agents that I knew to form a cohesive program. Bringing people together for the sake of shared resources and experiences is crucial for BIPOC writers. Community solidarity is one of the best ways to combat oppressive structures and gatekeeping.

If you are a solitary writer or find that because of work, family obligations, access to transportation, etc. and you can't meet other writers in person, there are many critique groups that meet via Zoom or online once a month or once a week. Many are very flexible with attendance. If you are better in a bunch, there are a great number of writing organizations that are now beginning to safely meet in coffee shops or libraries. With social media it's fairly easy to find any of these groups but there are other platforms like MeetUp and EventBrite that specialize specifically on creating local groups and events for people around specific interests.

While working in publishing and writing during my free time over the years, I found that there were many communities for writers, but not many that centered on BIPOC authors. In fact, I could not find one when I first began my search.

This is important. White supremacy is real. It is ingrained into every part of society, not just here in the U.S., but beyond. So much so that those who benefit do not even realize it and, at times, do not understand that some of their criticisms of the writing of BIPOC writers are also criticisms of their culture. An example of this is having to italicize non-English words which often has the effect of making us think that our native tongues are "other" when, in fact, many of these languages are native to the land prior to European colonization. I'll never forget when I joined a writing group in Redondo Beach, California. There were about 10 people in that group, all white except for myself and a man of Filipino descent. His story was rich and layered with connections to his culture in a fantasy setting. My stories tend to encompass a lot of ties to my Latinx culture with folklore and a world filled with magical realism. In that group, he and I received the most criticism because the rest of the people in the group did not "understand" the culture of the worlds we had built. Nor had they tried to look up any of the references we wrote. To them, they simply didn't get it. Yet so many of us are expected to just "get" their references to WWII or to English idioms. We were looked down upon for not understanding European references, but we were expected to make our references entirely understood to our white counterparts. The constant justification of our cultures and writing wore us both down and when he stopped showing up, so did I.

I didn't write much after that. There was no moment of declaration, but I think that subconsciously I tired of fighting for my culture to be heard. The one good thing that did happen in that group was that an unsaid camaraderie developed between that writer and me.

During my search for writing and reading communities, I settled on one that, whilst it was made up of predominantly white women, there was at least one other non-white woman there. I felt a sense of safety since we were both there and we already knew each other. There was an unspoken vow to support each other in our efforts to modernize and diversify our chapter. My abuela always told me that sometimes in order to make changes that matter in systems that don't work for your community, you have to infiltrate them first. Then you can make the changes from the inside out. This is what I did when I joined the

Women's National Book Association. Slowly, my colleague and I made changes to bring more diverse programming to our chapter and recruit more members who were representative of our community. This not only took time, patience, and courage, but it also took understanding that there would be push back because many people do not like change. There were times when we would vent to each other about micro-aggressions or outright rude and ignorant comments, but we stayed focused and worked even harder to create whatever change that we could. Fast forward to a few years later and we have both served on the organization's national board, overseeing all eleven chapters. I am now the current president of the entire organization, the first Latina president of the 105 year old organization, and I founded and run our organization's first DEI (Diversity, Equity and Inclusion) initiative, the Authentic Voices Program.

Through this program, I mentor and bring resources and education to BIPOC communities with a writing, editing, and publishing masterclass. Not only do the fellows who complete the program get published in an anthology, but they receive a stipend towards the cost of the program, and learn the necessities and business side of publishing. The program is in its third year and our past fellows have gone on to work in many areas of publishing and as well as attaining representation from agents. This program, that has changed lives, might have never existed if I hadn't taken a chance on being uncomfortable for a bit to make a change. Real change can be made as long as you will it to happen. All it takes is that first step.

Get to Know and Apply for Writing Opportunities

In my work mentoring BIPOC communities, I've noticed that our communities are the first to second guess ourselves when it comes to the merit or value of our work. Meritocracy is perpetuated by the gatekeepers. I have met so many AMAZING writers who don't understand how amazing their work is and think that it isn't as valuable as the writer holding an MFA.

That is absolutely wrong. I know many great storytellers who have never had access to educational systems. Because of this, their stories go unfinished. You do NOT need a degree to have merit. In fact, there are opportunities for BIPOC writers to get paid to write! All you have to have is a good story to tell.

Various organizations, including Women's National Book Association, provide free programs to writers. Many of these programs take place online and are recorded in case you can't make it to one. While the Women's National Book Association is membership based, with a fee that ranges from thirty to fifty dollars per year depending on which chapter you join, the value is beyond measure. It is within the Women's National Book Association that I could discuss the need for DEI measures and get support for the Authentic Voices Program. It is also within the Women's National Book Association that I made lifelong connections in the book world. Programs within our organization such as the Authentic Voices Program, specifically for BIPOC authors, are open to non-members and pay participants a stipend. Organizations such as the Women's National Book Association are always presenting opportunities for writers to get to know all the different avenues of writing and publishing so you can make informed decisions about your future in writing. Women of Color Writers is another program that gives free resources focused on BIPOC writers. There are now dedicated organizations looking to help get more diverse stories out there, so take a look and see what you find.

Support Other BIPOC Writers

Publishing is like any other business, it needs to see a return on investment. What this means for you is that the more you support BIPOC writers by purchasing their books, writing and leaving reviews, sharing their books on social media, etc. the more publishers are going to continue to open the doors to BIPOC writers. While it may seem vast, publishing is a small community. Chances are if you are in constant support of BIPOC authors, they will find out who you are, and when it comes time to celebrate you, you better believe other BIPOC writers will repay the favor. Follow your favorite BIPOC authors on social media. Engage with them in their chats about writing. Compliment their work and let them know the feelings it evoked. BookTok, Bookstagram, and Twitter are great resources to find BIPOC authors to support. There are specific podcasts dedicated to highlighting BIPOC authors as well. Listen to those to learn from various authors about how each of them overcame obstacles and got their book published.

There is a saying in Spanish, "Hoy por ti, mañana por mi." Today for you, tomorrow for me. This is how I have lived my life in publishing, one day at a time for me and for you—my community. Take time to make today for you and your writing and storytelling. Take the time to celebrate those who have had publishing success. One day that person will be you.

Top 10 Countdown for BIPOC Writers AND Our Allies

10. Know that while the publishing world was inherently set up to focus on white stories and authors, many publishers are now trying to right their system's wrongs. Because of this there are many panels and opportunities that publishers are now setting up in their attempt to create equity on book acquisitions. Search for those opportunities by signing up on various publishing houses' websites for their newsletter.

9. Because of the courageous work of many in publishing, the search for BIPOC authors has expanded into many levels of publishing. There are agents who are actively searching for BIPOC authors to represent and have made that known on their manuscript wish lists. Do your research on Manuscript Wish List and see who is looking for your type of story.

8. Tell Imposter Syndrome to take a hike. You CAN be a writer! Chances are, you already are. A writer writes, that is all that's required. You are the ONLY person who can tell your story, and I can bet someone wants and/or needs to read it!

7. Discard antiquated thoughts that creativity cannot make you money or a living, however, take time to get to know what white counterparts are making so that you are not taken advantage of. Follow hashtags like #publishingpaidme to get to know the state of some of the financial aspects in publishing.

6. Join and/or create writing communities that are familiar with or willing to learn about BIPOC stories without making it "the other."

5. As long as your safety is not impeded in any way, don't be afraid to join groups that make you feel somewhat uncomfortable. Sometimes, if we have the strength, organizations have to be shown where they might be lacking in DEI and you might be the perfect person to lead the way in those discussions.

4. Apply for writing fellowships. Fellowships with adequate funding and committed to equity now offer stipends and scholarships for BIPOC writers.

3. Support BIPOC writers. They walked so we could run. Make sure you keep the doors open for your own stories by supporting other authors from BIPOC communities and showing publishers that our stories sell.

2. Take time to celebrate your writing and how far you've come.

1. Enjoy the process.

Meet Natalie Obando

Natalie Obando is a graduate from California State University, Long Beach with a BA in journalism emphasizing public relations and a minor concentration in creative writing. For nearly two decades, she's worked in the world of books as a book publicist. Natalie is the founder of Do Good Public Relations Group and the author of *How to Get Publicity for Your Book*. She is the current national president of the 105 years old non-profit, the Women's National Book Association (WNBA), overseeing all eleven chapters across the nation. As the first Latina president of the national organization, her goal has been promoting diversity in publishing via strategic grassroots efforts. She is also the founder of the grassroots organization, Women of Color Writers Podcast and Programming. Her dedication to promoting diversity, equity, inclusion, and belonging in the book world led her to found and chair Authentic Voices—a four-month long program that immerses people from marginalized communities in a master class of writing, editing, marketing, and publishing.

Natalie has spoken at some of the most well-regarded literary conferences in the industry including the The West Coast Writers Conference, the Central Coast Writers Conference, Publishers Group West Conference, as well as conferences that focus on diversity in publishing such as Centering on the Margins.

Always looking to amplify BIPOC writers and create community and discussion around diversity in publishing, she recently joined the Ladderbird Literary Agency team. As a literary agent, she hopes to further usher BIPOC writers into careers as authors.

Instagram: @wocwriters
Website: www.womenofcolorwriters.com

Own it! You are a Business!
Stephanie Larkin

"Can anyone really make any money selling books?" for authors everywhere, this is the age-old question. While a million factors go into the eventual answer to that question, it is important to understand how money IS made in books. This means you need to understand a bit about royalties, retailers, discounts, and other items that will affect your profit possibilities. The fact of the matter is that if you are choosing to publish your book, you are opting into an agreement that you, as an author, are running a business. Now, much of that has to do with marketing which is covered in the third book of the *Launch Pad* series, but here, it's time to explore the ins and outs of how authors make money, and they do!

First, full disclosure: while there are many reasons why a person should publish a book, I generally wish for the first-time authors I work with to set a non-financial success goal for their book. I want the new author to be proud of the enormous accomplishment that writing—and publishing—a book truly is, and not to be discouraged by sales numbers. Nothing grieves me more than a new author who is flying high on a cloud after a book launch to plummet radically when their book is not an instant bestseller, and their royalties are more on the level of "buy a latté" than "buy a car." I so hate to see the light go out in their eyes as I remind them that this is their first book, and no one wins the Olympics on their first run down the ski slope.

Yes, there are many authors making a living on their writing, and that is a wonderful vocation. But new authors sometimes forget that those authors also went through growing stages to get where they are today and expected huge financial successes for themselves with their first book, which is rather unrealistic.

So, what goal IS there for writing a book other than money? Honestly, most new authors never even thought about the money at all while they were writing—they were simply inspired, excited, enamored, or even plain obsessed with writing their book, and often couldn't sleep until their book was completed. It isn't until after publication that the concept of return on investment (ROI) even enters their mind. When their book isn't producing instant financial success, it manages to deflate their confidence and ego like a lead balloon.

We write because, as Toni Morrison stately so eloquently, *"If there's a book that you want to read, but it hasn't been written yet, then you must write it."* We write because we can, because we come alive through the pages, because our characters are begging for a voice, because writing is like breathing—we simply cannot NOT write. Money is great, but creative literary expression trumps it any time!

I can hear you saying, "That's all fine and good, Stephanie, but please get back to the subject of making money!" Okay, here goes, some nuts and bolts about royalties, retailers, discounts, and more, so that you can set realistic goals, maximize your profits, and go forward with full disclosure.

Royalties

Book royalties are another word for profits from sales after the publisher has taken their percentage. Royalty receipts are the first and ultimate "what's in it for me?" An author receives royalties from a number of sources in a variety of ways:

A self-published author receives royalties directly from the retailer or aggregator they used to publish their book. A self-published author may choose to publish directly to online retailers such as Amazon/KDP, Barnes & Noble, Google Play, or other online retailers, in which case they will receive royalty payments from these sources. They may also self-publish through an aggregator/distributor such as IngramSpark or Draft2Digital, and then receive royalties from them, as well. Traditionally and hybrid published authors receive their royalties directly from their publisher. In this case, the publisher is receiving the royalties from a variety of sources and then sends them to the author.

Audiobooks also receive royalties, and these can come from a variety of sources just like book royalties. Authors who produce and self-publish their own audiobooks may opt to publish directly to online audiobook retailers, such as Apple or Amazon, or may use an aggregator such as Captivate. Additionally, many audiobooks are produced—and subsequently published—using Amazon ACX, and thus royalties will be issued by ACX.

When does an author receive royalties?

Different retailers and aggregators pay out royalties anywhere from 30-120 days once a book is purchased. Traditional presales of books available on Amazon or Barnes & Noble do not actually pay out to the author for those presales until 60 to 90 days after the release of the book. While retailers and aggregators often report on book sales much closer to the actual sale date, the payments for those sales don't follow for months afterward. This could certainly cause financial strain if you are running expensive ad campaigns—even if they are working beautifully, you will be paying for the advertising months before you receive the fruits of those sales.

How are royalties calculated?

In general, the equation for overall royalty calculations goes something like this:

(Retail price - % which goes to the distributor/retailer) - print price = your royalties.

So a book that retails for $10 with a print cost of $5 sold on Amazon (and Amazon generally takes 40%) would be like this:

($10 - 40%) - $5 = remaining royalties.
10 - 4 - 5 = $1 remaining royalties.

Yes, Amazon gets $4, and you get $1. Please note that Amazon takes their percentage BEFORE removing the print costs, which makes it a higher percentage. The same formula will apply whether your book is sold on Barnes & Noble or any other online retailer. IngramSpark takes 30%. For digital books, the good news is that instead of subtracting the print cost, the equation would subtract the download cost, which is much smaller—often under $1. Plus, retailers often take a smaller percentage on a digital book. Amazon currently takes 30% off a digital book that is priced between $2.99 and $9.99, but 70% from a digital book priced below $2.99 or higher than $9.99. Therefore, if a book had a download cost of $0.75 (which is paid to Amazon along with their percentage), here is how the royalties would factor if the book retailed at $9.99 and if the book retailed at $10.

($9.99 - 30%) - $0.75 = remaining royalties.
9.99 - 2.997 - .75 = $6.25 remaining royalties.

- Or -

($10 - 70%) - $0.75 = remaining royalties.
10 - 7 - .75 = $2.25 remaining royalties.

You can see why it is vitally important to understand how royalties are calculated, as it may play a critical role in the pricing of your books and how you choose to market them. Certainly, you can see how much more lucrative digital books can be over print books, and you may consider that when planning advertising or other promotional strategies.

Amazon also has KU—or Kindle Unlimited—which is a program where subscribers pay a monthly fee for unlimited access to books enrolled in the Kindle Unlimited program, and authors are paid by the number of pages that are read by subscribers. DC Gomez has a terrific chapter in this book all about Kindle Unlimited, which can help decide if KU would be a good fit for your book and potential readers.

With all things having to do with pricing, it is important to check other books in your genre and comparative size so that you have a good idea of pricing expectations for your buyers.

Who else gets a "bite" out of your royalties?

If you are a self-published author, all remaining royalties go to you. Of course, for the sake of planning, you should calculate any of your various marketing activities including ads, travel to book signings, table rentals, postage, and any bookish "swag." Since you will be marketing in a variety of ways, calculating the ROI of any one method individually would be impossible, but it is still worth checking your royalties vs. advertising to be sure you are indeed profiting from your books. We more fully discuss marketing in book three of this series.

If you have a publisher, then your publisher receives your book royalties and then shares your percentage with you. Your percentage may vary from 5% to 95% depending on the publisher, so it is important to read your contract. Some publishers may quote you a flat fee—such as "you'll receive $1 per book sold at retail"—but it is a good idea to understand how royalties work so that you may compare that rate to others as a percentage.

Audiobook narrators may be paid a lump sum for their part in the production of your audiobook, or may prefer to take a percentage of royalties - often 50% - instead of an upfront payment. Additionally, if you have an agent, an illustrator, or any others who have contributed to the publication of your book, they may be assigned various percentages of the remaining royalties, as well. These may range from 2-20% and sure can add up, so you will want to watch your royalty report—and better yet, your publishing contract—with an eye toward your actual split.

Retailer Discounts and the Power of ISBN Numbers

If you are traditionally published, your publisher will have agree-ments with booksellers everywhere both online and in stores. Those agreements are beyond your control.

If you are an Indy author, the widely-preferred term for self-published, you have options—herein the power of registering for multiple ISBN numbers. The ISBN, of course, is the identifier of not only your specific book but every version of your book. Yes, your eBook, audiobook, and print book all have separate ISBNs. Additionally, if you publish with Amazon/KDP, you have their number. But it's also important to have a registered number with IngramSpark, and here's why. Most bookstores will not place a book on their shelves if they cannot first make a profit and second return it if it does not sell. A bookstore is not going to buy a book from Amazon. They don't get a discount. Bookstores need retailer discounts.

What exactly are "discounts" for retailers? When a bookstore purchases copies of your book from IngramSpark or another distributor, they receive a discounted rate—generally between 40-55% off. For example, if a book that retails for $10 is purchased by the bookstore at a discounted rate, such as 40% off, they would purchase their books at $6 each. They are then able to make a profit on your books. Many booksellers will not stock your books with less than a 55% discount—acquiring your $10 retail books for $4.50—which can certainly eat into any profit, and could also leave the author "upside down" owing more than they make. Additionally, most stores will not order books unless they are able to return unsold books, and the cost of returns is charged to the author, as well.

Be sure to set your sale prices so that you have enough margin for all expenses while remaining appealing to your buyers.

Can I sell my own books?

Absolutely! As an author, you have access to "author copies" of your book. This will be laid out in your contracts across plat-forms. You are assigned a flat rate for the purchase of your book, and if it hasn't been said before, you have to calculate how many books you want on hand for giveaways and events. Once your author copies are in your hands, you have full rights over costs and distribution. All of this factors into the all-important ROI of being an author. However, selling your own books directly to readers at book fairs, talks, workshops, and other events should be planned. You can even sell directly to local bookstores, gift shops, and specialty stores that are somehow themed or linked to the themes and messages in your book. There are many advantages to author sales over relying upon online retailers, including:

- No lost "cuts" of royalties to retailers, which is often the biggest financial loss of all
- Direct contact with buyers, which can lead to more communication, upsells, and a better understanding of your reader base
- Control over all aspects of the buying process, including price, promotions, coupons, bundles, autographs, and more.

Selling books directly to buyers entails stocking inventory—purchased at the most competitive rate—and fulfilling orders yourself. (Here you will see the most profit and control but also take on the most work.)

Alternatively, you can use a service to handle fulfillment and shipping, resulting in smaller profits and less control, but less work, as well.

You will also want to participate in book giveaways. These are often done as part of social media promotions. Here, too, however, you will want to consider the value vs. expense of these events. Gifting an eBook is one thing, but if it's an in-hand copy, there are costs involved. In this example, you have purchased your book at the author cost and now also have to ship the book. If you include bookmarks, note cards, or other swag, there are those costs involved, as well.

Just a side note here on monies earned through your book sales. All monies earned are subject to your local and federal tax laws. This is also true of books you sell at events.

Keep very specific records of all your expenses related to the sale of your book such as trips to the post office, print shop, or speaking engagements, as well as the cost of books you purchase. In like manner, if you engage an individual to provide services to you in the area of marketing, distribution, etc., you may be required by law to issue them tax documents reflecting the cost of these services.

Although these expenses may appear substantial, rubbed against royalties and sales profit, they will ultimately result in higher ROI. In short, keep track of all spending for ads, publicists, swag, equipment, computer supplies, subscriptions to professional organizations and services, and every cost you incur related to the publication and sales aspect of your work. It's never too late to meet with and engage an accountant to discuss your author life and the implications on tax filings and profits.

Kickstarter

Kickstarter is a crowd-sourcing website that helps to fund many new products, artistic endeavors, and an array of other ideas requiring capital. Head over to kickstarter.com, and you will find everything from prototypes of new technology, unique designs and fashion, and off-Broadway plays trying to get off the ground. Kickstarter has become a major player in the publishing arena, as well, and many authors use it to raise funds to pay for their publications in advance.

Here's how it works. Visit kickstarter.com and explore the site to see if it is a match for you. If that's a yes, set up a Kickstarter campaign at no charge. There you can upload images, videos, and text about your upcoming publication. You can also set up different "reward" levels that sponsors will receive for their contribution. A Kickstarter campaign for an upcoming book usually includes rewards for different book formats, including digital books, softcover books, hardcover books, and signed limited editions. Authors can also offer additional items, bundles, services, or even appearances as different reward levels for contributors.

In this way, a Kickstarter campaign can entice people to become sponsors, purchasing a book from an author even before a book is available to the general public. This way, finances can be raised even before your book is completed, and production costs can be paid out with money raised through presales on Kickstarter.

How else can I make money from my books?

Believe it or not, the best way to make money as an author is to write more books. Books beget books and sales beget sales. Historically, it is sometimes an author's third book that "kicks in" and results in sales. These sales then springboard and rejuvenate the sale of previous books. This is, in part, a result of well-developed author platforms (we address this in book three of this series) but also because readers are now eager for your work and sharing about it.

Depending upon the type of books you write, there are many other ways to make money from your book aside from retail book sales. While not all apply to every type of book, perhaps there is one below that would be a good fit for you and your author business.

Paid Speaking Engagements

While exclusively an outlet for non-fiction writers in the past, even fiction writers can manage to branch out from author to author/speaker. Brainstorm on topics you may enjoy speaking about that dovetail nicely from your book, topics in writing/publishing, or a more motivational angle focusing upon embarking upon the arduous journey to authorship. Rotary and similar civic organizations, as well as many clubs, regularly look for speakers.

And of course, a speaking engagement can be rolled into an opportunity to sell books directly to participants—either at a table at the end—or a guaranteed book purchase for each participant by the sponsor.

Classes and Workshops

If your speech topic has room for expansion, offering a class or a workshop could be a great way to dive deeper into your subject area, increase your fees, and sell more books. Workshops can be online or in-person, ranging from half-day to multi-day events. If such a workshop can be recorded and adapted into an online course, your possibilities for making money and selling books increase, even when you are busy with other things.

Bulk Sales

If selling one book is good, selling thousands is earth-shattering! Depending on your subject matter, there may be corporations, organizations, or other opportunities for bulk sales of your book. Brainstorm on ways that others may benefit, and present possibilities such as:

- An inspirational book used for corporate gifting
- A location-based book for the travel industry in that particular area

- Children's books for schools, shops, or children's organizations
- Books highlighting a medical issue for doctors, hospitals, or non-profits focused on that condition.

The sky's the limit (at least in your imagination) on how your book could be integrated into the programs of an outside group. This could bring you bulk sales in which you set your own prices with no royalty splits—a win-win for all!

As you embark upon your publishing journey, remember that monetizing your book is a marathon—not a sprint—and that by exploring various options, you can find a way to enjoy the journey ... and hopefully some profits as well! Many, many authors make a respectable living as writers. You can, too, but it will take planning, hard work, luck, and you continuing on your writing journey. Write!

Top 10 Countdown to Making Money Writing Books

10. Check other books in your genre and comparative size so that you have a good idea of pricing expectations for your buyers.

9. Be sure to set your sale prices so that you have enough margin for all expenses while remaining appealing to your buyers.

8. If bookstore sales are an important part of your sales strategy, be sure to set discount rates and return policies as needed.

7. Shop around for competitive print pricing to secure your own book copies for in-person sales.

6. Remember that shipping costs can decimate your profit margins quickly, so evaluate potential shipping methods and materials with an eye toward process, packaging, and profits.

5. Brainstorm about what speaking opportunities can lead to direct book sales while expanding your author platform.

4. Consider ways to multiply your own book streams of income, including online courses, direct sales, and workshops.

3. Securing bulk sales can get your book out to readers faster than individual sales.

2. Brainstorm about unconventional ways your book can dovetail with other organizations or even products, and present a proposal to decision-makers to show them how such a partnership would benefit them and support their goals.

1. Remember that the best way to sell more books is . . . to write more books! Not only will your sales increase simply by having more books available for purchase, but each book will also "boost" the others so that the effect of more books is indeed greater than the sum of their parts. Happy writing!

Meet Stephanie Larkin

Stephanie Larkin is the "head penguin" of Red Penguin Books and Web Solutions, an independent book and web publishing company for over 15 years. Stephanie is the host of television's *Technically Speaking*, an award-winning educational cable TV series airing in Queens and Long Island, *The Author Corner*, airing on Verizon and Optimum, *Between the Covers*—the show for readers, writers, and lovers of books, and her podcast *Once and Future Authors*, available on Spotify, Apple Podcasts, and other podcasting platforms.

Stephanie's goal and company motto is "Changing lives ... one book at a time!"

Website: RedPenguinBooks.com

Picking a Publishing Path
Valerie Willis

You have finished your novel, edits are done, your manuscript polished and publish ready, and now you need to decide how to get your book into the hands of readers. This means you need to pick your publishing path. There are so many options from traditional, author services, small press, and self-publishing. Choosing one comes down to each author's needs and wants. It's important to know in today's market that an author can create their own success no matter which path they use, but here are some facts to be aware of upfront.

If you want full control of the entire process, decision-making, and final say on any aspect of your book—*self-publishing is the only way to obtain this.* Being successful at self-publishing will always take a balance of time and money with the mindset of you the author are the business, your books are your product, and readers are the consumers. This means finding services and contractors that can make covers, line and copy edit, type-set/format your book, and more. Yes, posting through large vendors like Barnes & Noble and Amazon can be done free for eBook and Print-on-Demand, but making a competitive book takes some sweat and tears, and time and money.

For the sake of this discussion, let's first focus from the perspective of you deciding to go "traditional" as they call it in the wilds of literary land. This doesn't mean you are only pitching to the "Big 5"or "Big 20" publishers such as HarperCollins, Macmillan, Simon & Schuster, Penguin Random House, and so on. This also includes pitching a variety of big publishers, midsized companies, small press, literary agents, and even editorial departments.

The first step is being aware there are plenty of pay-to-publish companies out there including vanity and hybrid presses and author services who often paint themselves as traditional publishers. Yes, they are publishers with similar reach, but it's how you land a contract with them and the contract terms that can leave an author in debt or paying a lot out of pocket upfront. That being said, it doesn't mean these aren't options if you know what it is you want out of them and manage to negotiate a contract that fits your needs.

In the end, you should be able to identify a "traditional publisher" by three core principles:

- Neither traditional publishers nor literary agents ever ask you to "pay to publish" or pay to lock into a contract. If you are asked to do either of these things, you are working with a hybrid press or author services firm which includes (past and present) AuthorHouse, Xlibris, Xulon Press, Mill City Press, and more. Be aware, some companies may even require a submission process that mimics the same methods of a traditional publisher, and after "accepting" or "reviewing" your manuscript and/or query letter suggest what package is best for you. This may be a viable option for your manuscript, but it is not traditional publishing.

- There's a vetting process that requires you to submit a query letter, book proposal, or use a submission form of some kind. It should feel like you're about to apply for a job, and in a lot of ways you are! The traditional method that has been in place for *a very long time* is to submit a query letter and sometimes a small sample of work.

- Traditional publishers never approach an author first or do cold calls to let you know they saw your book and wanted it. Unless you sold THOUSANDS of copies, it's very rare. These calls often declare they have been following your book, or did marketing research on your book, and feel it's "a good candidate to publish" with them. Sadly, this conversation segues into them asking you to pay to lock into a contract and eventually pay to publish. I still get these calls on old short stories I self-published over a decade ago despite now owning a publishing company!

Query Letters and Process

Perhaps everyone keeps telling you to "query," or make a "query letter," but you're not sure what on earth this really means for you and your book. In short, think of it like your book's job resume for potential employers, or in this case, publishers. This letter plays an important role for the publisher, editor, or literary agent who is reviewing it. It's designed not only to introduce you and your story to them, but also to serve as a snapshot of how they would need to market this book for the long term. In short, it helps them answer one of two questions: Publishers: "Can I sell this?" or Agents: "Do I need one of these for my list or know a publisher looking for this?"

It's not uncommon after an author lands a publishing contract that the query letter is sent to a marketer or marketing department to help them know how to place this book within the publisher's catalog, design the book cover to match genre and audience, and decide on keywords for searchability before releasing the title. Be mindful, this doesn't guarantee you will be chosen or included in high-dollar marketing efforts as most publishers are choosing manuscripts based on trends, audience, location, and more to pick the book in their inventory lists that has the best chances to succeed in a certain season or marketing venture. Some books may never get ads via their publisher's channels, so always know the AUTHOR is the best chance at letting readers know their book is in the world.

Your query letter should be comprised of three main sections:

- Introduce your book, your audience, and what makes this something they would invest their own money and time into. This often includes your book title, target audience, word count, genre, and similar information. The idea is you want them to know how aware you are of what kind of book you are trying to get out into the world and who your reader is so they can envision what your book will compete beside and share an audience with.

- A blurb, pitch, or market-savvy product detail that describes the main character, love interest or antagonist, and the type of story you are pitching. Sometimes this is just a paragraph, but following current trends of how marketers write a blurb can go a long way. There are even copywriters who specialize in helping create these for an inexpensive price! A solid blurb should outline the goal, motivation, and conflict of your main character, love interest, and/or antagonist. Through this information, the publisher should clearly recognize the genre, the potential audience interest, as well as what makes your book unique and trending for its intended reader.

- Tell them who you are and why you're the best person to tell this story! This is where many authors struggle the most. They want to see a short bio about you as a person and writer. Listing awards and memberships to associations is helpful but shouldn't make up the majority of this part. Instead, you want to let them know you are active in the writing community and on social media. If you come from a community that would invest in the story, share that, as well, i.e. I wrote a medical thriller and I'm a doctor, too! Just make sure that what you create can't be mistaken for your obituary!

Example query letter:

Dear [AGENT or PUBLISHER],

Love's Hellhound is a Paranormal Romance Comedy complete at 75,000+ words with series potential. It captures the comedic dialogue of the movie *The Mummy* (starring Brendan Fraser) but with the paranormal flair from Sherrilyn Kenyon's *Dark Hunter* series. The story takes us to an urban fantasy setting reminiscent of our own world and bounces between the two love interests, Isobel and Arael.

Is a reanimated hellhound undead? Alive? Or undead undead? Alive undead?

Dr. Isobel Shipton manages the night division at a local supernatural veterinarian office and when Arael Lionhart walks in with a hellhound who's eaten a holy relic, it's as if the billionaire bachelor walked right off the cover of "Paranormal Times." Unable to save his pet, Isobel is appalled that Arael seems more concerned about his brother killing him than over the loss. Later that night, Isobel accidentally revives the hellhound with newfound necromancer powers, chasing the hellhound all the way back to Arael's townhouse.

Arael seems to have been expecting her, and chemistry starts to spark between them. The two come to an understanding; the dog stays with Arael, but Dr. Isobel will be making daily house calls because how can she not make sure the hellhound is going to be ok? Scandalous articles say, "the doctor is in, and the bachelor is out." Isobel's powers grow with voyeurism through the hellhound just in time for Arael's shower, communing with dead relative's spirits, and summoning forces which may land Arael in a family feud like no other along with a bigger secret about Arael's true identity that might send Isobel over the edge.

Valerie Willis is the COO at 4 Horsemen Publications, Inc., an expert digital typesetter, co-host of *Drinking with Authors* Podcast, and an award-winning fantasy paranormal romance author. Her works include a workbook series, *Writer's Bane*, starting with *Research and Formatting 101*, and novels inspired by mythology, superstitions, legends, folklore, fairy tales and history such as in her *The Cedric Series*. Many have experienced her hosting workshops or being a guest speaker at events where she shares her expertise in publishing, novel writing, research for fiction, world-building, character development, book design, reader immersion, foreshadowing, and more.

Thank you for your time and consideration.

With those things in mind, be sure to take your time and really treat these query letters no different from a resume. Be sure to change who you are addressing to match the sender. If the literary agent or editor you've written the query letter for favors certain genres or themes they are looking for, be sure to tweak the letter to bring those items forward in the overall tone of the letter.

From a publisher's perspective, please be sure to review submission guidelines and requirements. First impressions are everything in this industry and receiving an entry via email or submission form that doesn't answer the questions at all or fails to follow directions is an automatic rejection. It tells them you can't follow directions nor understand the information needed for future endeavors since the author-publisher relationship is a partnership. That job resume vibe is even here at this stage because this is answering, "Are you qualified and capable of doing the job asked of you?"

Be mindful, querying is a slow process for both sides. Publisher and agents often take a lot of time to reply, answer, or reject. In my own ventures, these time frames vary from ten-minute formal rejections to a year later being asked for a full manuscript to be reviewed. This all comes down to the publisher or agent and how many letters they receive. Often a question at panels, senior literary agents can receive 100-300 emails per day. That's a lot! So be kind, be patient, and know this is not intended to be a fast process.

You have a letter but now where on earth do you look to send this out to agents and publishers. Or perhaps you want more insight and help to create your letter. Here are some resources.

- QueryTracker—a website that lists publishers and agents. Free to use with paid access to extra features. Links to websites, comments from previous authors' submissions, and a great snapshot of what is happening now.

- Publisher websites—often they may have a submissions page or instructions on how to do so. They will let you know what they are seeking or keep it generic.

- Literary agent or agency website—will always tell you what genres they represent and hope to get in so you can cherry pick the best one for the best chances.

- Submittable—popular software/website for literary based or similar companies and anthologies.

- Poets & Writers—a great in the know place that often lists agents and publisher as well as what is happening in the industry.

- Pitch or query events—connect with your local writing crowds to discover when agents, editors, and publishers will be hosting these. It's a great chance to pitch your book in person and get feedback.

- Conferences and conventions—often you can attend a session or pay to get access to industry experts. Again, a great way to meet these experts in person and get feedback on a wide variety of fronts or pitch your book.

- Workshops—this is a great resource for having an agent or editor in the seat to help you create a strong query letter, review first pages, and more. Often these intimate workshops are limited to 5-10 people, and it's a chance to tighten up your letter before doing a mass querying attempt.

Building a Reputation

Even if you haven't finished drafting your story, it can't be over emphasized how important building your reputation is for the modern author. Why? Because this can factor into how successful you are as an author as well as how appetizing you look on a query letter. This means reaching and keeping a growing list of readers and fans that later fuel reviews, sales, and word of mouth for you and your books is vital (and required whether you self-publish or traditionally sign with a publisher/agent).

No, you don't need a finished manuscript or published book to make this happen. Since 2017 to the present day (even through the pandemic!), Ingram (one of the largest book distributors) and Written Word Media (a well-known book marketing resource for authors) have both reported that the top three ways people discover a new book or author include: word of mouth (readers and book clubs), author platform (author newsletter, social media, and events), and SEO, or Search Engine Optimization (publisher's ability to utilize ONIX system to tag on a program keywords and information or metadata that runs behind the scenes on vendor websites). In short, it takes all three to be successful! Start building up your reputation before and during querying.

Many new authors who are being signed in recent years have often stated they already established many of the following:

- Newsletter—this is the most powerful author tool to date. 10-20% of the active subscribers will buy books and/or leave you reviews! *Personal Note: Early in my career I hired a marketing consultant to assist where I was failing on marketing my book. I was missing a newsletter, added one in January of that year with 16 reviews on Amazon, and by December, I had 60+ reviews on Amazon and a permanent increase in organic sales!*

- Social media—choose one that fits your genre that you feel comfortable using. Most of these now allow cross sharing and you can pull them to where you are more active. Making reader groups, hosting book and author events, and learning the hashtags that get you in front of your audience are great ways to connect with future readers ahead of time.

- Blog—sometimes these double as a newsletter. Having a place where you share progress and samples of your work to hook them can be a huge help when first starting out with no publications under your belt. Let your writing sell itself!

- Website—having a convenient place where readers can go to find where they can connect with you can be vital. This can house your blog, collect newsletter subscribers, link to all your social media, and even keep events and releases in one place.

- Book clubs and reader groups—take part and become familiar with your future readers through clubs and groups both online and in person. Learn from them and get their support. They will help you get off the ground and get word out there faster than anything else in the market. These are great for helping with book launches! Using inner circles to reach outer circles is a great starting point for your own author events.

- Associations, memberships, and guilds —connect with similar writers and authors. Readers are voracious and read multiple authors and books in the same genre, so feeding the machine is a group effort. Having connections or being part of certain groups shows you're investing in this career track and learning from proven sources. It's not uncommon that once new authors are signed, they are encouraged or obligated to join organizations because they provide aid (health insurance even!) your publisher will not be able to give you, such as assistance in marketing and continued education. Some suggestions include Author's Guild, Independent Book Publishers Association, Women's Fiction Writers Association, Florida Writers Association, and more.

- Conferences, workshops, and events—look for events that vibe with you and your intended audience. Whether it's the local comic con, book events, or even the flea market, get out there and interact, scope out what in-person events you want to be part of, attend or participate in panels and workshops, and keep your fingers on the pulse as a writer.

Literary Agent vs. Publisher

Going down the traditional path comes with options as well. The biggest divide is choosing whether to query a publisher or literary agent (and you can query both sides if you are willing to give either a shot!). There are pros and cons to both, but at the end of the day, it falls back to the individual author to choose which fits the relationship and interactions you prefer to encounter throughout your career as an author or during the life of your book and its contract.

The Agent

Literary agents are like the mortgage brokers of the publishing world. Granted, each one is slightly different. Some will work as part of an agency while others may be independent. Regardless, they often have a shopping list of what they know is trending or that publishers have requested and will often search to find a book that "fits their list." That doesn't mean they won't pull something they like or feel they can push, but know that this shopping list is the foundation or underlying goal of an agent.

Many books are auctioned to an array of publishers. That means they will put your book into an auction for the highest bidder to win and contract out. Often an agent will inform an author this is happening and lay out terms in advance. Much like a broker, they take their cut out of the royalties and advances once a book is signed on with a publisher. The other side of this is many agents will negotiate better contract terms, but it's recommended to always have a contract lawyer on hand to help you decode the fine print no matter who you are dealing with because *that responsibility falls on you the author to protect yourself.* Agents will often offer a more personal and intimate relationship compared to a relationship with an editor at a publisher. Each agent is different with different policies, so be sure to go in with an idea of what you hope to get back out of an agent.

Landing an agent is the same as a publisher, through the querying process they will sort and vet manuscripts. As I stated before, agents can receive 100-300 emails in a single day in peak seasons or when there are trends influencing submissions. The first wavee of rejection will always be one of two matters: "Did the author follow directions and submit according to the guide-lines?" or "Is this on the list of items I need or want for pitching to my publishers and at auction?" Again, this doesn't mean they won't see a story that they resonate with and want to give it their best attempt to pitch. The next wave will most likely be based on how clean both the query letter and manuscript are which will fall to: "Did they do their best to catch simple spelling issues and grammar flags?" or "Does this query letter entice me to read?"

After this point, you may get a request to see more! A partial request will come with a specific page count, chapter count, or word count. As for a full request, this means serious consideration, though you may not be in the clear on rejection, as they need to read more. Sometimes they are doing soft inquiries of the story with all their channels to see if there's any interest. Often a rejection at this stage comes with a more informative reply or personal rejection. That doesn't mean you won't get the rejection of "doesn't fit my list" because no interest could be seen when they looked into their channels. Know it's not beyond your reach to ask the agent at this point if they know someone who would be a good fit since they've seen the full manuscript.

A relationship with an agent usually includes coaching. They often assist their authors with booking shows, marketing, continued education, access to guilds, and more. That being said, there may be different levels of contracts or even outside services they can provide. They will pull from their already signed authors for a publisher's needs for a story before taking from the query pile which essentially gives you an edge and opportunity for future work. Just remember that a bad agent or even public relations rep is on par with getting a bad tattoo artist. It may make future endeavors difficult and it's something that doesn't "wash away" so easily. Be sure to investigate and ask authors about their experiences and recommendations.

Publishers and Presses

Publishing on the traditional side means the backing and established channels from a publisher will make sure your book has a greater reach (than if you had self-published selling books to libraries, large retail chains, etc.). However, you will get limited if any say over cover, interior, edits, and more (some smaller presses will let the author give feedback, but this is the minority). You will need to be understanding that the publisher has a vision for your book, and it may not match your own at all. For example, the award-winning Nancy Springer, author of *Enola Holmes,* once jokingly told me she didn't understand why she got a crime/mystery book award because she writes fantasy. Needless to say, she has movies on Netflix now! You will have to trust the publisher's vision for your book.

Granted, there are some publishers out there who share mockups and get feedback or author input, but don't take it personally if they bypass any that you provide. At the end of the day the publisher is making a product they can sell, which in turn, means getting your book in the hands of readers, which in turn leads to royalties that allow you to keep writing. There is a level of patience and trust that needs to pass between both parties when you step into a relationship with a publisher. Agents and publishers often imply signing a contract is like marrying someone, and you should make choosing and reading the fine print vital steps. (As previously mentioned, contract lawyers are great resources for this step).

Yes, you can query directly to a publisher and press. Depending on the company, this can be hard to do or a preferred method. Some work exclusively with a select few agents while others don't work with agents at all. Regardless, the querying process is overseen usually by an editor, editorial department, or even a special department or entity. Much like the agent, publishers use a similar process to weed through the queries and submissions.

Unlike the agent, publishers usually have a manager or editor in charge of authors and correspond through them. These representatives work as liaisons in most cases. Authors rarely work directly with any of the teams. Despite that, it doesn't mean you can't develop a close relationship with the editors and certain individuals you encounter through a publisher.

Contracts get more aggressive here on a publisher level. Again, it can't be repeated enough the importance of seeking a contract lawyer in cases where fine print and rights are involved, especially when money is being exchanged. Not every contract will have money paid up front in the form of an allowance or advance. In most cases your royalties must "pay" this amount back and the standard contract is three years from the book's release date. An advance or allowance is often a means of implying they are buying exclusivity and you can't publish elsewhere or comes with other stipulations. Other times this amount is so they can "buy the rights" of the series and any likeness.

Be wary of contracts that leave open-ended clauses in the publisher's favor. For example, a common one to review is "First Rights of Refusal" where often the author can get in huge trouble for not bringing their next project to them. Upon a "no," the author may do what they want or follow guidelines as defined in the contract of what they can do with a spinoff or another book idea (again, watch wording to keep things to the book and series, be wary of author-defined barriers). If a contract doesn't say how long before it's considered an automatic "no" from the publisher, guess what? That means they don't have to ever reply, and you can't do anything about it.

Another common publisher-side red flag is anything dealing with selling rights to third parties. These often have clever underwriting that makes it so that they can "sell your translations/audiobook" to a "third-party" and no longer are obligated to pay you royalties from those books. It's a scary tactic, and it's been seen from small press all the way to large publishing imprints including large licenses or brands at big commercial companies. These contracts may remove you from any rights beyond the initial book itself, like merchandise and media.

The lines between big and small publishers have gotten a little muddled with recent changes in the industry. It used to be that a big publisher had a better chance of getting your book into large retailers' physical stores. Now, we find books sold by both big and small publishers side-by-side on tables at Barnes and Noble! Thanks to digital and print-on-demand leading the way to sustainable printing practices, small presses can distribute through the same channels as large houses. It's also not uncommon for new and upcoming publishers and presses to be bought out by the "Big 5."

No matter the path, know that the best option comes back to what you want for your book and yourself as an author. How much control, time, money, and type of relationships you want to build and maintain for the duration of the experience is completely in your hands.

Top 10 Countdown to Picking a Publishing Path

Your path to publishing is for you to choose. This key advice should make that choice easier.

10. Get to know the publishing industry, what it offers, and your options.

9. When in doubt, get a contract lawyer involved. Even as a publisher, I often encourage folks to review my own contracts thoroughly because I want them to be very aware of what they are signing.

8. You will always need to market because you are responsible for letting the world know you have a book in the ocean of books. Only you can guarantee your own success.

7. Don't hesitate to ask for help and educate yourself on all elements of the agent/publisher relationship, including asking for recommendations for publisher, agents, and more. Keep a finger on the industry pulse!

6. Finish writing the book first! You can't make a choice without first having the book completed and in hand. In short, don't skip ahead in making decisions and causing distress that leads to writer's block.

5. Become familiar with online tools and networking resources.

4. Never skip on the editing process. It's vital and shows you're serious and aiming to be a professional. The more publish-ready your manuscript, the more appetizing it looks to a publisher and agent.

3. This is a job interview! First impressions go a long way. Be professional and concise, let them know who you and your book are, and where you fit in with them and the world.

2. Follow directions and guidelines. Don't be the reason you are rejected and self-sabotage by rushing in without considering what is being asked of you and your work.

1. Your query letter is your best calling card.

Meet Valerie Willis

Valerie Willis is the COO at 4 Horsemen Publications, Inc., an expert digital typesetter, co-host to Drinking with Authors Podcast, and an award-winning Fantasy Paranormal Romance author. Her works include a workbook series, *Writer's Bane,* starting with *Research* and *Formatting 101,* and novels inspired by mythology, superstitions, legends, folklore, fairy tales, and history such as in her *The Cedric Series.* Many have experienced her hosting workshops or being a guest speaker at events where she shares her expertise in publishing, novel writing, research for fiction, worldbuilding, character development, book design, reader immersion, foreshadowing, and more.

Website: www.WillisAuthor.com
Instagram: @WillisAuthor
Facebook: facebook.com/ValerieWillisAuthor
Twitter: @Valerie_Willis
TikTok: @willisauthor

Audiobook Ambassadors
Theresa Bakken

Crossing paths with wordsmiths is one of my perks of being an audiobook narrator. After just a few years in this field, the community of storytellers I find myself in is as complex and varied as the stories they stitch together. And yet, I've found the desire to shine a light on other people's work and make time for each other has been universal. So, I was not really surprised at the kindness I found when I went looking for audiobook guidance from some industry giants. With the help of generous authors, producers, audiobook publishers, and narrators, I've gathered as much wisdom per word as I could find. I hope you will hear them out, and then see them as ambassadors with open doors.

Let's start with why you should care. Here's some data to preface the personal perspectives and insights.

According to the Audio Publishers Association's Sales Survey conducted by InterQ, publishers' audiobook revenue grew 25% in 2021 to $1.6 billion, which marks the tenth straight year of double-digit growth. Nearly 74,000 audiobooks were published in 2021, a 6% increase over 2020. Science Fiction and Fantasy narrowly edged out Mysteries/Thrillers/Suspense as the most popular genre by percentage of sales, with Romance and Fiction following close behind, and increases in Children's and Young Adult revenue. This year, the romance genre experienced the most growth with a 75% increase in revenues, followed by self-help (34%), and science fiction (32%).

Additionally, Edison Research conducted the Audio Publishers Association's 2022 Consumer Survey and found: The percentage of Americans 18+ who have ever listened to an audiobook is now 45%, up from 44% in 2020. Membership in audiobook services increased, with 41% of listeners indicating they subscribe to at least one such service. And, 54% of audiobook listeners are under the age of 45.

If you're still skeptical, author Robb Grindstaff knows the feeling. Robb is a novelist, short story writer, fiction editor, former journalist and news media executive. He has three novels with Evolved Publishing, a fourth one coming, and has published more than twenty short stories. He also has a chapter on editing in this volume. Here's what he told me about his slow warm up to audiobooks.

> *"I delayed moving into audio for several years. I didn't really understand the draw. I'm not an audiobook listener. I made the mistake of thinking if I don't listen to audiobooks, then no one else does, right? Wrong… My publisher prodded me occasionally, and then, over time, I started getting more and more readers and potential readers asking if and when my books would be out on audio. Some said, 'The only way I read books anymore is on audio. Let me know when yours are available.' So I caved in. And yes, I should have done it years ago.*
>
> *What I wish I knew then, and what I hope authors today realize, is that readers have options and different media and methods that*

they prefer to engage with books. How you read may not be how someone else reads. Some still want to hold that book in their hands (like me). Some love reading on their devices, whether laptop, Kindle, cell phone, whatever. And some want to hear the book read out loud on audio. **Make your work available in whatever medium readers want or you're missing a segment of the audience."**

So, I asked Robb about the specifics of his and his publisher's audiobook process. Here's his answer.

"For me, with a small publisher, I have to invest in audiobooks personally. Therefore, a revenue share is about the only way that makes sense for me. I'm not going to sell thousands and thousands of audiobooks. If I sell a few hundred, that would be amazing. But as a writer and a freelance fiction editor, I completely understand that artists (including voice artists and narrators) need to be justly compensated for their time, efforts, and expertise. I don't have the voice or experience to narrate my own novels any more than I could design a front cover or run a major publicity effort. I have to hire professionals who know what they're doing to support my writing in these critical areas.

My publisher generally works one of two ways: a lower upfront cost plus a percent of audiobook royalties, or no upfront costs and a larger percent of royalties. This helps to keep the initial investment to something us starving authors can afford. If the project is successful and the audiobook sells well, then both the author and the narrator win. The narrator can wind up making more than the flat fee."

This is a good place to throw down some audiobook contract acronyms and definitions. Robb brought up two kinds of audiobook contracts—RS (Royalty Share) and RS+ (Royalty Share

Plus PFH). PFH stands for "per finished hour" and refers to an hourly rate for the finished hours of the audiobook. PFH rates can vary widely with narrator experience, accolades, and popularity. Most narrators have a history with all the different contract formats, and they have criteria for how they choose which is best for them.

For perspective, I asked a professional narrator with hundreds of titles in romance, bio/memoir, YA and literary fiction. Andi Arndt is a member of the Audible Narrator Hall of Fame, and a search of her name on Audible turns up over a thousand results. This is because in addition to narrating, she is also the Founder of Lyric Audiobooks which produces award winning audiobooks for best selling authors. Another feather in her cap—she is the founder of a tremendous resource for narrators seeking professional development and fun. It's called Narrator.Life. Here's what Andi Arndt said about how she chooses an RS vs. a PFH project.

> *"I have done very few royalty share (RS) projects. The most successful have, at their core, an open, collaborative and trusting relationship between me and the author. I like to know how the author plans to promote the audiobook. If I get the sense that the author is passing the lion's share of the risk and up-front costs to me, it's unlikely I would accept an RS+ offer because I have enough PFH work that it doesn't make sense to trade a sure thing for a question mark."*

I've heard echos of what Andi just said from many narrators. How we choose RS and PFH projects is a risk and reward balance, a business decision, that is tempered by a gut feeling about relationship and collaboration. **Understanding the pros and cons of the different contracts for your audiobook project is essential.**

Next, Andi opened a door for me and introduced me to the Executive Producer at Lyric Audiobooks, Katie Robinson. And, Katie provided her perspective and author tips for audiobook success.

> *"I think there is no one way to succeed in publishing audiobooks, but there are certainly a few ways to try to help things along! One of those, just like any avenue of business, is market research. Do you have the sales in print/eBook to help support your investment into audio production? Request (from a producer) or calculate an (audiobook production) estimate and **evaluate how many audiobook sales you'd have to make in order to earn out.**"*

I wondered if Katie thought audiobooks were a good investment for Indy authors. Here's her answer.

> *"Absolutely. We all know that audiobook publishing is a growing industry and nowhere is that more evident than in genre fiction: mystery, romance, scifi, and fantasy. The best part is, you don't need to be traditionally published in order to reach listeners in those categories. Romance audiobook consumers in particular are (in my experience) the most devoted, high-consuming, fan-involved, and narrator/author-loyal fanbase; that's part of what makes it so fun and rewarding to work in this genre. The major thing is that authors have to be just as devoted as the fans —authors can tap into that market by caring about those listeners, producing high quality work, and ensuring wonderful performances."*

So, I asked Katie what she would like authors to know about audiobook timelines for casting and production.

> *"This is probably the most common question I receive—'how soon can I produce an audiobook?' The answer can be slightly compli-*

*cated. The biggest factor in our timeline is narrator schedules. **If you're working with a popular narrator, you'll often need to reach out at least 6 months ahead of time** (some less, but some more) to secure a spot with them. At that time, authors won't need to have the manuscript, but they should have a few details about the book like an estimated word count, character background to ensure representative casting, and any other info they're able to provide. I always tell my author clients, the sooner you can get a book on my radar, the better—and the more likely we are to be able to cast your favorite narrator(s). If authors are in a rush and are open to working with narrators who may not be quite as busy, we can always try to find the right fit right away.*

Once the manuscript is in-hand and the actual production process begins, things can move very quickly! Lyric Audiobooks can have audio over to you for beta listening within 2-3 weeks. But it's always good to keep in mind that narrators are people who (just like us) sometimes get sick or have random loud construction happening next door that can delay the timeline a bit."

Along these lines of setting expectations for authors, I reached out to another producer for answers. This is Craig Hart, Executive Producer at LRT Media.

*"One of the common misconceptions is that the finished product will sound exactly as it did in the author's head. **An audiobook is a completely different medium than the printed page, and it's best to hire professionals in that field, and let them make the best product they can.** That may echo what the author heard in their head when writing, but often it may not. Sometimes authors try to be the directors of their projects, and that rarely ever works out. Don't micromanage. Hire the best you can, and let them do their jobs."*

Because Craig has experience casting narrators and also works as an audiobook narrator and voiceover artist, I asked him about finding the right narrator for a project. Here's his advice for authors auditioning narrators.

> *"When listening to auditions, try to listen beyond the voice itself (although that is important), and focus on how the narrator is telling the story. It's easy to get blinded by the sound of a voice— negatively or positively—and either miss real talent or excuse weaknesses. Remember, **not all listeners will have the same immediate reaction to a voice that you have, and so it's best to choose based on the storytelling ability of a narrator and not simply their tone or timbre.** "*

Because I know Craig has produced and performed in a variety of audiobook formats, I asked him about projects with more than one narrator—duet and multicast projects.

> *"Duet and multicast projects are growing in popularity but are also more expensive to produce. Generally speaking, I think **duet and multicast are best for pieces that have an inherently more theatrical feel to them, and where the author is fairly sure the production will recoup the additional expense.** "*

My next source of sage advice is an actor, playwright, novelist and audiobook narrator. He particularly enjoys working in multiple accents and lifting the drama off the page. I reached out to him because he has narrated his own novels. Here's Chris Humphrey's advice for authors who want to take that self narration route.

> *"I would caution most authors against attempting to narrate their own novels. (Not because I am trying to get more work!) But it is quite the skillset—vocal training, sight reading, technical expertise if you are using software and editing/mastering yourself.*

*People who consume audiobooks have very high standards and even if an author is a gifted amateur, someone may well not buy the book if the sample doesn't hold up. That said, if someone really feels they want to attempt it, I would get the Hindenburg software (one month's free trial) and give it a go. There's a little learning curve but not as steep as many systems and the support is very good. You'll need to read articles on how to create the studio space —soft furnishings work well, I essentially record in a duvet fort. Then **record a few chapters and get opinions.** Not perhaps from family and lovers—you will need unbiased feedback: is this the sort of vocal delivery of this material that you would wish to listen to for twelve hours?"*

I then asked Chris how he picks projects to narrate. Here's his direction for Indy authors and small publishers who are looking for narrators like him with multiple distinct character and accent skill sets.

*"You can put up auditions on both ACX and Findaway Voices. State the sort of voice you would like, the variety of accents etc. And the cost. Some narrators will work on profit share (RS). I never do. As they say: you get what you pay for. Truly, I would listen to narrator's 'tapes' (samples) on those sites or, perhaps even better, just search Audible for books like yours and listen to the narrator's sample. Can you hear your words spoken in their delivery? But word of mouth is always good too. **You can track down a narrator pretty quickly these days and send a request.** I get nearly all my work that way—people recommend me after I've done their book. It's very nice!"*

My final source is famous among narrators. Karen Commins is an award-winning, professional audiobook narrator, producer, publisher, writer and leading curator of information about the audiobook industry. She's the chief cartographer of NarratorsRoadmap.com—the destination for narrators of all levels seeking answers and professional development. She's created an Audiobook Distributor Comparison Chart which analyzes six distributors across 22 points. She also writes a blog for authors and has created two pages of audiobook resources to help authors. (You can find all the source links at the end.)

I asked Karen to chime in on a topic all narrators are talking about: Members of the Audiobook Steering Committee of SAG-AFTRA (Screen Actors Guild-American Federation of Television and Radio Artists) and board members of PANA (Professional Audiobook Narrators Association) are circling the wagons and urging narrators to get educated and involved. The issue we're discussing passionately is AI enabled audiobook narration. Here's what Karen has to say about the new technology.

> *"Many small publishers and authors are considering using artificial voices to reduce expenses. As a professional audiobook narrator, I'd like to offer some important points that authors should consider before embracing a synthesized voice to record your books.*
>
> *One's voice conveys the essence of being human. Nothing expresses our thoughts, feelings, and emotions better than the human voice. Calling Alexa and Siri "artificial intelligence" is really a misnomer. These devices and apps may sound sort of like humans, but they truly "just read." They are not capable of thought and do not have life experiences that will shape and color a performance.*
>
> *Devices do not take breaths. Without breath, you have no life. In fact, listeners have said they grow uncomfortable if they cannot hear the voice taking a breath.*
>
> *These two simple but profound differences prevent artificial voices from being a suitable choice for any long-form narration, but especially not for an audiobook that is competing with other forms of entertainment for consumer dollars.*

Authors carefully choose every word they write. Audiobook narrators work to understand each word and make organic acting choices that convey the author's intent. We can change our rhythm, volume, pitch, intonation, tempo, and pauses. We give fictional characters a unique inner life and instill vibrancy into non-fiction texts. In contrast, an AI voice can't imbue any word with meaning. It can't detect the subtext in a single sentence, much less over the trajectory of an entire book. Experienced narrators actively mine the subtext for clues and create a more expressive, layered performance based on it.

A narrator can say the same sentence in a number of ways to impart different meanings. For example, the listener can actually hear the difference when I smile! How would an artificial voice understand the underlying humor in the text and say the words so that the joke lands? It can't.

*When an author considers everything she'd lose by choosing an AI voice over a human voice merely to save a little time and money in audiobook production, I'd hope she'd realize that **the true value in an audiobook is in the human narrator's ability to tell the story and take the listener on the journey with us.** "*

I think that image of a journey we are all on together is so perfect for this storytelling community. I want to thank Karen and all the industry ambassadors who responded when I called and asked for help. And I want to thank you for listening to what we had to say. For more, just follow the links to everyone you heard from in order of appearance.

Theresa Bakken: https://theresabakkennarrator.com/

Robb Grindstaff: https://www.robbgrindstaff.com/

Andi Arndt: https://www.andiarndt.com/, https://narrator.life/

Chris Humphreys: http://www.authorchrishumphreys.com/

Katie Robinson, Lyric Audiobooks: https://www.lyricaudiobooks.com/

Craig Hart: https://www.narratorsroadmap.com/

Karen Commins: https://www.narratorsroadmap.com/, https://www.karencommins.com/blog, Audiobook Resources for Authors, Audiobook Marketing Cheat Sheet, Audiobook Distributor Comparison Chart

Top 10 Countdown

10. The true value in an audiobook is in the human narrator's ability to tell the story and take the listener on the journey with us.

9. You can track down a narrator pretty quickly these days and send a request for an audition.

8. An author interested in recording their own audiobook can find help with the technology, but they should also get honest feedback on their performance with a sample recording.

7. Duet and multicast are best for pieces that have an inherently more theatrical feel to them, and where the author is fairly sure the production will recoup the additional expense.

6. Not all listeners will have the same immediate reaction to a voice that you have, and so it's best to choose based on the storytelling ability of a narrator and not simply their tone or timbre.

5. An audiobook is a completely different medium than the printed page, and it's best to hire professionals in that field, and let them make the best product they can.

4. If you're working with a popular narrator, you'll often need to reach out at least six months ahead of time.

3. Evaluate how many audiobook sales you'd have to make in order to make a return on your investment.

2. Understanding the pros and cons of the different contracts for your audiobook project is essential.

1. Make your work available in whatever medium readers want or you're missing a segment of the audience.

Meet Theresa Bakken

Theresa is an Emmy Award winning journalist. She brings warmth and wit to every project and is often cast in Cozy. She also shines in armchair travel, loving language and accent work. Her Texas roots easily come out in southern storytelling. And, she brings her love of audiobooks to the Desideratum Podcast with insightful author conversations produced around sections of their audiobooks. She records from her home studio in Colorado, where she lives with her husband, her honey bees, and a small barn full of feathered and wooly friends. Her three grown children inspire, encourage and remind her that each chapter in life builds on the last and opens new doors.

https://theresabakkennarrator.com/

https://linktr.ee/tbnarrator

The Right and Wrong Ways to Get Published

Erika Lance

Now that you have started this chapter with that headline you might be ready to skip to the part where I tell you the right way to get published. Are you ready for it?

Drumroll . . .

The right way is the way that actually works best for you and your goals.

It depends on the time you have, how willing you are to learn new things, and to be frank, your personality. This is not earth-shattering news, but something that I recommend is that you take some notes on what you want out of your publishing journey as you are reading this chapter and the rest of this book, as your publishing journey will be more satisfying for it.

Not sure if you noticed but I did not say that your publishing journey would be easy. I often make the analogy in writing to the finding of Marylin Monroe. She was working at a factory, and a photographer took some photos, and Norma Jean ended up being discovered. However, if you think you will be sitting in a Starbucks and one of the top editors from one of the big five publishers is going to see you typing away, walk up and ask you about your book, option it on the spot, and give you six figures, you need to keep reading this book, many others, and listen to the many podcasts on the subject.

So to start off, one of the first things you should do is decide what you want out of being published. Is it just a book in your hands? Is it for friends and family? Or do you want to be as famous as Stephen King or George R.R. Martin? This will tell you how to go about publishing.

On my podcast, *Drinking with Authors*, I have discussed the publishing journey with hundreds of authors. I can tell you that it is not easy and it is absolutely different for everyone. It is, however, rewarding.

So where should you begin?

Some Interesting Statistics

If you are starting your journey, there are some realities that you need to know in order to set the right expectations. Here are some recent statistics published by Bookscan.

The following data shows print sales over the last year (52 weeks), ending 8/24/2022 from seven of the top publishers in the world. This data is for 45,571 books sold.

0.4% (165 Books) Sold over 100,000
0.7% (320 Books) Sold between 50K and 99,999
2.2% (1015 Books) Sold between 20K and 49,999
3.4% (1572 Books) Sold between 10K and 19,999
5.5% (2518 Books) Sold between 5K and 9,999
21.6% (9863 Books) Sold between 1K and 4,999
51.4% (23419 Books) Sold between 12 (Yes, it said 12) and 999
14.7% (6701 Books) Sold under 12.

It would be great for you to read this again. I did not include this to dissuade you from your writing/publishing journey. I instead want you to understand the reality of the publishing industry.

There was also a very informative hashtag that was trending on Twitter a couple of years ago: #whatpublishingpaidme. I would look this up, it was very informative and gave insights into how the different ways publishing a book can and does pay.

When you are publishing a book, you are now a business. This is an important factor most authors do not understand. You are in the business of selling your books, regardless of how you are published. This is something you need to think about as you begin this journey.

There is also another factor in publishing you should consider which is series or multi-book based writing.

Another statistic over the last twelve years or so shows that the "real money" starts to come in when you are at book six. This might seem like a lot of books to write, but if you write every day, even for twenty minutes, you will get faster and better at it and more of your creativeness and imagination will be out there for readers to read.

Many readers get done with a good book and immediately look for what else that author has written. I know I am disappointed when I find out that there is nothing after that wonderful book.

There are groups of writers, the most famous that I know of is 20Booksto50K, that specialize in this method of making money for writing a series (or multiple series). This is done by self-publishing your books. Which brings me to what method of publishing is the right one.

Let's begin with, what I would say is the most crucial thing to understand in your publishing journey, which is: What type of personality do you have? The reason this is most important is simple. If you need to have true control over everything, there is no publisher on the planet that will give that to you.

Needing to have control is NOT a bad thing. However, you will find that if you are not willing to let go and allow the publisher to do what they believe is right, then you will have a very frustrating, unhappy journey.

Let's now discuss the ways you can be published.

Self Publishing

Self publishing used to have a terrible stigma, some think it still does. It used to mean you could not get your book published, usually because it was assumed that your book wasn't any good, so you had to do it yourself.

With the advent of websites like Create Space (the name before Amazon purchased them) you could suddenly not only create your book, but you could also list it for sale on websites. Previously self published books were run off on printing presses and at copy shops. Now they were able to be done more quickly and look more professional.

The other issue with self publishing, which is one that unfortunately is still rampant today, is that some authors do not run the book or manuscript through a good editing process. Many new authors tend to think their words are gold and that they need little to no editing. Or they think they can have someone they know "edit" their work. As most of the prolific authors will tell you, a good editor is someone who is first and foremost trained to do editing and second willing to actually edit your work. Stephen King had a new editor assigned to him that was afraid to edit him and one of his books came out with a bunch of errors that a good editor would have caught.

So, regardless of how you decide to publish, get your book professionally edited. There is no faster way to lose your audience than for your work to not be edited.

There are a few types of editing you may need:

- **Developmental editing** can help ensure your story is the story you want to tell that your audience will not be able to put down.
- **Structural editing** makes sure the story flows correctly and that the scenes and reveals are in the correct order. This can usually be done as part of developmental editing.
- **Line editing** to make sure your grammar, tenses and punctuation is correct.
- And finally **Proofreading** which is a final pass to make sure there is nothing missed and you did not change Sally to Sarah.

After editing, true beta readers will be the final step so that some very fresh eyes take a look at your words. They are also wearing the hat of a reader so they will find those little things the editors and you have missed.

If you decide to go the self-publishing route, make sure you educate yourself on the true cost of things such as covers, typesetting, editing, proofreading, etc. The publishing business, like most others, has people who will take advantage of you. If you do not know what you're asking for and how much it should cost, then you could end up spending thousands of dollars and not have a book worth that.

Controlling every aspect, or self-publishing, also means you will have to get yourself fully in the know of what genre you fall into. Or as they call it in the biz, the BISEC codes (BISEC: Book Industry Standards and Communications). These are updated at least annually and it is how you indicate where your book falls for readers and retailers. You would not want your steamy werewolf romance in a middle-grade or cooking category.

Some of the major plus points to self-publishing are:

- You decide when your book is published. You are not running on someone else's schedule.
- You decide what format your books are published in.
- You get to choose everything about your book. TOTAL CONTROL!!!
- You can make a larger percentage of your sales.
- You can publish just to apps.

Here are some of the potentially negative points to self-publishing:

- The distribution of the book can be more limiting. You have to upload it to most retailers, such as B&N, Amazon, Kobo, IBooks, etc. yourself.
- You have to get pricing right to get into retail outlets (such as brick and mortar stores or libraries). They expect at least 55% discount on books and the ability to return.
- You are fronting 100% of the costs.
- It is time consuming. You are doing everything, so you need the time to learn how to do it all, or find those people who can do it for you.
- You do not have anyone, but you, keeping you accountable. This goes back to the whole personality question.

This is by no stretch of your imagination a complete list, but some things to think about.

Agents

An agent can be the best, or potentially best, partner you can have in getting yourself published. Some of the large publishers will not even look at your manuscript unless you have an agent. As publishers, however, do your homework. Who have they represented? What kind of deals do they negotiate? How quickly do they usually get contracts for their clients? What genres do they represent? What percentage do they take from you? How long is your book tied to them? Are you tied to them for ALL publishing?

You have to be very careful to read the fine print as to what they are going to do for you, what you are giving up, and for how long. This is where I would also encourage you to use a contract lawyer.

Getting an agent can be exciting, however, if you cannot publish anything unless they shop it around, that might stunt your ability as an author.

This is an area where you need to get references from authors who have worked with the agent. Do not ask them who you should reach out to. Make sure you make the choice who to approach, and speak to several authors.

Another point to research is their reputation since they will be your voice. Is it the right voice to speak for you?

Like publishing this can be a marathon, so prepare for the time it will take and the possible rejections.

Traditional Publishing

Most people think that traditional publishing means that you are published by the "Big 5" large publishers. This, however, is not the case. There are many small to medium publishers that are fantastic and give what could be considered the traditional publishing experience.

If you are looking to go the traditional publishing route, I suggest you have a completed and polished manuscript. This means that it has run through an editing process. This does not mean that you will not be edited by your new publisher. It does give you an experience with the editing process and will help you see some of the things you need to work on for further books. Most importantly, however, it will allow those publishers you are submitting to not be thrown off by some of the issues of first time writers (such as switching tenses).

When looking at a publisher, you want to look at what they publish. Do your research. This is a point I cannot stress enough. Look at the types of books they publish. What do the books look like? How are the books doing in rankings? Do they have more than one book per author? If you are a series-based author, this could become very important. Then, if you find a publisher you are thinking about submitting to, reach out to their authors and ask what it is like to work with them. Reference check them! It is important to know who you would be giving your art to.

I have heard a ton of stories about how the author has never actually met the publisher (or their editor). All communication is handled by email.

There are horror stories of publishers not paying royalties. Find out from the authors if they received any royalty payments.

When you are ready to submit, be prepared to wait. Most publishers take quite a long time to get back to you. Be prepared; this is a marathon and not a sprint. There will also possibly be many rejections. Stephen King kept them on a nail in his office, and there were over a hundred and fifty. Being rejected does not mean you should give up. It means it might not be the right book for them at that time. If you are lucky, the publisher will give you some feedback on anything they see that needs to be improved.

When you do get the opportunity to speak with the publisher about publishing your book, and I recommend that you insist that you do, here are some things to ask:

- What medium do they publish in? Do they do paperbacks, hardcovers or audiobooks? I know several that only do eBooks.
- Where are their books published? If they say they are on Amazon and B&N, that is not even a fraction of the vendor possibilities.
- Do they copyright your work? If so, do they copyright it in your name? If the answer is no to either of these questions, walk away. There are so many authors who cannot do anything with their work because it is owned by someone else.
- Do they file with the Library of Congress? This is not a huge deal, however, it is a way to have your work be located in what is considered *the* US Library.
- Do they want to charge you anything to publish? If they do, they are a hybrid press. See the section below on this.
- What is the royalties schedule? This is important to understand when you may see money for your work.
- What is the term of their contracts? This is important to understand how long you will be in a relationship with them, even for just that book.
- How long will they keep your book published for? And if they un-publish it, what happens to the rights?
- Can you get author copies at a wholesale price? I know one author who was made to pay retail cost for his books. He ended up buying used copies off of eBay.

- What rights do you have regarding the choice of covers and title? There have been so many books where the title and covers were decided solely by the publisher and the authors had no recourse. I will tell you that a good publishing company will have final say on a cover or title, but will want to work with the author to create a book they love (and at the same time is marketable).
- How does the editing process work? One of my guests on the podcast told me how the publisher made them switch genders of the lead character and then changed the ending. There will be some give-and-take to get the best story out, but it is your work, your voice, your art. Do not let them take it from you.
- How long will it take for your book to come out? I have heard that it can take up to 4 years. Are you willing to wait that long?
- If they are offering an advance, make sure you find out the terms. Most advances have to be paid back if the book sales do not equal or exceed that amount.

The above are some of the points you should ask but not all.

If you are offered a contract, have it read by a lawyer. Yes, this costs money but you need to fully understand to what you are agreeing. This is another point where you may lose the rights to your own work. You may also be agreeing to publish all your work than with them. This could lock you into a corner with no legal recourse. Contracts are not set up to protect the author, they are set up to protect the publisher. Remember that no matter how nice they are you need to protect yourself.

I find that when authors finally get offered a contract they are so thrilled that someone wants to publish them, that they forget that they are the artist in this deal. You need to make sure your art and your voice are protected, so be prepared to walk away. There are always other options.

Hybrid Publishing

To be fully transparent, I am not a huge fan of an author ever having to pay to get their books published. Traditional publishing is an intimate relationship between author and publisher where the traditional publisher takes on the financial costs and risks and partners with the author to ensure their manuscript comes to life. There simply aren't any costs to an author for that partnership. Traditional publishers make money when you, as an author, are successful.

Today, there are so many publishing options open to authors that author services firms and hybrid presses have flooded the publishing marketplace. Author service firms are just that. A company that has been formed to create a variety of services from cover design to loading a manuscript on digital platforms. These firms are decidedly not publishers, but are a path for some to have their words in print.

Hybrid presses on the other hand, offer a still different path to publishing. If you find yourself in a position where the publisher wants you to pay for your cover, typeset, editing, etc. these are the marks of working with non-traditional publishers. A word to the wise, if you are drawn in this direction, do your homework. Research the company, their books, the quality of their publication, and what authors say about their experience with this press. You will want to make sure you understand all aspects of what the hybrid publisher offers including marketing and editing services. It is likely that the hybrid press has a variety of publishing packages to choose from at a variety of services and cost levels. Critical to your study will be the distribution reach of the hybrid press to get your book on multiple media platforms and in bookstores. Equally important, is how the press makes its money after your book is published. Do they have a vested interest in your success, not only on a personal level but for their own business model?

If you go in with eyes wide open and the hybrid publisher is transparent in their contract, costs, and author services, and with a proven quality product that you can be proud of, then this may be a good match for your manuscript. Remember the numbers we have discussed above about how many copies of books are sold.

All of the same questions that were laid out above for publishers apply to this method. Then, the biggest thing to look at is how much can you spend on your writing craft. I will remind you that you are in the business of selling your books. One of my favorite sayings is: "Is the juice worth the squeeze?" It is important to really look at all of these things before signing anything.

Are you stuck with one publishing choice?

The quick answer is no. You can do self-publishing, traditional, and also hybrid for your various books. Try different routes and find what works best for you. This is a journey and you have to be willing to change your mind about the right course.

There is so much education on the topic of publishing. You have started with this book, which is amazing but don't stop. This is important, and with anything important, it is worth doing right. So, learn all you can so you are making educated decisions about what is right for you.

You are amazing!

Top 10 Countdown to Finding the Right Way to get Published

10. Look at what method of publishing works best for you.

9. When you get that publishing opportunity remember to take a deep breath and understand everything about it. This is your art.

8. You are in the business of selling your books. Approach everything you do from that angle.

7. Consider all your publishing options. Traditional publishing asks for your personal partnership, not a financial one. Traditional presses are options well beyond the Big 5 publishing houses. Hybrid presses may be a viable path for but ask for you to make a financial and a time investment beyond traditional presses. Self publishing gives you total control, but it requires you to carry all of the responsibility.

6. Listen to the experts and find what works for you. There are so many who have been where you are now.

5. Be patient; it will happen. You just need to remember that the process is not a reflection on you or your art.

4. Find an agent and/or publisher who wants to be a partner with you in your publishing journey. You should all be on the same team.

3. Continue to learn. Do not stop even after you are published. Knowledge is power.

2. Make sure you get legal advice on any contracts.

1. Have fun with this journey. You are creating something amazing and through all the twists and turns, never lose sight of that.

Meet Erika Lance

Erika Lance is a writer of horror, suspense, Sci-fi and a little fantasy. She has been many things in this life, but she is most proud of being a nerd before it was cool. Growing up in the 80's and 90's she will tell you, finding another female D&D player was rare.

She is also the CEO of 4 Horsemen Publications, Inc. and Accomplishing Innovation Press. She is also the host of the Drinking With Authors podcast and the co-host of Eerie Travels podcast.

Erika fell in love with the horror while watching Elvira and Dr. Paul Bearer on Saturday afternoon TV and was hooked. She believes that life is an adventure and it is built on the things you do, the people you surround yourself with and most of all the things you create.

She loves to create worlds and stories. Finding that not all stories have happy endings.

www.4horsemenpublications.com

www.drinkingwithauthors.com

www.eerietravels.com

www.erikalance.com

Insta - @authorelance & @drinkingwithauthors

Hybrid Publishing
Brooke Warner

I first started talking about hybrid publishing around the time I founded my press, She Writes Press, in 2012. I called it "third-way publishing" because it occupied a space that was not aspiring to be traditional, but was decidedly not self-publishing either—it fell somewhere in between.

Since then, hybrid publishing has exploded. In 2022, there are countless more hybrid publishers on the scene than there were a decade ago. With the entry of so many new players into the space has also come confusion and some bad actors. Because hybrid publishing is an author-subsidized business model, which means the authors pay for some or all of the publishing and printing costs, it's a breeding ground for companies that take advantage of authors by charging exorbitant costs and making hollow promises. As someone who runs two hybrid publishing companies and knows the value of this business model firsthand, my biggest mission and work as a publisher has been to educate authors so they don't fall prey to those opportunists.

Unlike the music and film industry, where Indy artists are expected to subsidize their own work—even lauded for doing so, in many cases—the publishing industry has been a real holdout, propagating a belief system that paying to publish is "less-than." Because I cut my teeth in traditional publishing (I worked for traditional houses for thirteen years before starting my hybrid publishing company), however, I know well the arbitrary decision-making of traditional houses when it comes to what they publish. You can have a gorgeous manuscript that rivals any other on a publisher's list, but if you don't have a strong author platform (online presence and many fans), they might choose not to publish you despite loving your work. They might choose not to publish you for reasons they will never tell you—because of something about you, like you're too old or you're not the right demographic (historically this meant because of your race or heritage, though in recent years many more writers of color are getting traditional deals). They might not acquire your book because they published something too similar too recently. And so you're at the whim of these deciding factors that have nothing to do with the quality of your book.

It used to be the case that after being rejected (perhaps once, perhaps many times), authors would pack their dream of becoming an author into the drawer alongside their failed manuscript—but the beauty of the current traditional landscape is that you don't have to do this anymore. Now any author can green-light themselves and become an author, and hybrid publishing is one of the paths forward on that journey.

Who's Right for Hybrid?

A good candidate for a hybrid publishing company is someone who wants to play in the same sandbox as their traditional counterparts. A reputable hybrid publisher will publish a book that's indistinguishable from a traditionally published book. They will also have meaningful distribution, and as such the author will also see more meaningful traction of their books into all sorts of sales channels, including online retailers, bookstores, and libraries. Publishing with a press with an already established reputation makes it easier for authors to get their books into brick-and-mortar stores and libraries, which of course results in broader sales opportunities.

Authors going the hybrid route must think long and hard about what they'll gain in relation to the money output. Hybrid publishers vary in terms of the costs of their publishing packages —as we go to press, these fees range from a low end of around $5,000 and to a high end upwards of $40,000. It's my opinion that serious authors who want to have a real shot at getting their books meaningfully distributed and who want a chance to be widely reviewed and well received are the best candidates for hybrid publishing. With this model, authors work with a publishing team that supports them in creating the best book, with the highest editorial standards possible.

Authors considering the hybrid route must consider their finances and know that it will be difficult to earn back all of their expenses, especially if they're paying on the higher end of the publishing package options that exist. Authors will earn back some money, but not all authors will earn back everything they invest. Understanding that publishing in general is both risky and competitive is essential. It's risky because it's a returns-based industry, so if books aren't selling, retailers can and do return them whenever they want to. It's competitive for reasons we all know—that there are so many books in the marketplace and not enough readers to go around. So setting your expectations, knowing what you gain for what your financial outlay is, will support you to have a positive experience with hybrid publishing —and to benefit from the meaningful gains hybrids can offer, which is broad distribution, legitimacy, and the possibility for being reviewed across industry outlets like Publishers Weekly, Kirkus, Library Journal, and Foreword, among others.

Good candidates for hybrid publishing are also those authors who have entrepreneurial spirits. When you hybrid publish, you are in essence a co-publishing partner with your publisher. You are putting forward the money to finance your book, which is an asset, and as such you want to think about how you're going to support the growth of that asset—through more sales. Authors who hybrid publish need to think about the long game—where their book and their sales are going to be in a year, in two years. They need to hire a publicist to get the word out about their book, because a book without a publicity plan is dead on arrival. (Yes, this means more expenses.)

It's a lot to take in, but the outcome of all this is a book that has the potential to reach many many more readers, and a publishing experience that brings you more visibility than you could ever hope to achieve via self-publishing.

What to Look for in a Hybrid Publisher

When I started my press, "hybrid publishing" wasn't a well-known term, even though plenty of publishers (even traditional publishers) have been cutting hybrid publishing contracts with authors for decades. So what we were doing wasn't codified. It felt like the Wild West, and it wasn't well understood. Because authors put up their own money to publish with us, some called us a "vanity" publisher, a term that's both outdated and always wielded as an insult. But a reputable hybrid publisher vets their manuscripts and has a rigorous submissions process. If a company does not have a submissions process, or if you as an author are being pitched their services—meaning they solicit you and not the other way around—they are not a hybrid publisher. Those companies are service providers. Some of those companies are good, decent folks supporting authors to publish; others, unfortunately, push authors to spend lots of money by catering to authors' weakness: the natural ego-driven desire to be told how wonderful their work is.

In short, be careful. If you are being pitched or sold to, you are not working with a hybrid publisher. A hybrid publisher has a submission process; they choose to publish your work based on an evaluation of your manuscript, or part of your manuscript.

In 2018, I worked in my role as a board member of the Independent Book Publishers Association (IBPA) to codify what it is to be a reputable hybrid publisher, precisely because so many companies were entering into the marketplace claiming to be hybrid publishers when nothing they were offering was actually what a publisher does. In fact, all they were doing was providing services, and as such we at the IBPA attempted to draw a bright line to differentiate between a hybrid publisher and a service provider.

I want to be clear—there is nothing wrong with working with a service provider. Companies like these can design you a cover and an interior. They can support you to self-publish your work, or sometimes even publish it under their own imprint. But this does not make a service provider a hybrid publisher. A hybrid publisher must vet manuscripts; they must have meaningful distribution; and they must have demonstrable sales. You can see the hybrid publisher criteria that IBPA came up with in 2018 and then revised in 2022 to add two additional points. If you're going to approach a hybrid publishing company about the prospect of publishing your book, make sure they're aware of the criteria and that they can assure you that they check the box on all eleven points.

IBPA's Hybrid Publisher Criteria
A hybrid publisher must:

☐ Define a mission and vision for its publishing program.
☐ Vet submissions.
☐ Commit to truth and transparency in business practices.
☐ Provide a negotiable, easy-to-understand contract for each book published.
☐ Publish under its own imprint(s) and ISBNs.
☐ Publish to industry standards.
☐ Ensure editorial, design, and production quality.
☐ Pursue and manage a range of publishing rights.
☐ Provide distribution services.
☐ Demonstrate respectable sales.
☐ Pay authors a higher-than-standard royalty.

Hybrid vs. Self-publishing

I shared above about the differences between traditional publishing and hybrid publishing, but what about the differences between traditional publishing and self-publishing? And why not just self-publish if you run up against those traditional publishing barriers? Good question.

There's nothing inherently wrong with self-publishing; the issue with this publishing path is that so many authors do it wrong and make mistakes. It's the old refrain: you don't know what you don't know. If you choose to self-publish, you'll soon discover that the term itself is a misnomer, because if you do it well you'll actually do very little yourself. Rather, you'll be hiring a team to support you to do everything from cover and interior design to converting your files for the e-pub version of your book to supporting you with project management.

The reason authors choose hybrid over self-publishing typically have to do with the desire they have for more access. Hybrid publishers (if they're legitimately hybrid publishers) will push their books into retail outlets, libraries, and specialty markets. Books will be warehoused, so you won't have to keep your inventory in your garage or fulfill orders from retailers like Amazon. Many authors also simply don't want to do the work of navigating the publishing industry on their own. It's helpful to have someone else hold your deadlines for you, tell you what to do next, and support you with the creation of the elements that will one day be your book.

Reasons authors choose self-publishing over hybrid often has to do with time. Self-publishing is faster; hybrid publishers will have a faster turnaround than traditional publishing. If a hybrid publisher has distribution to the trade, then the turnaround will never be as fast as self-publishing has the capacity to be. Distributors inherently slow down the publication process because of their sales force, and the fact that sales teams sell books into the marketplace six months prior to a book's publication date.

Self-publishing will also typically be less expensive than hybrid publishing. You're paying a hybrid publisher for certain services whose worth can't always be quantified—like reputation, sales history, and distribution. How much money you are willing and can afford to spend is an important conversation to have with yourself before you choose a given publishing path, always. Understanding the costs and what the potential earn-out scenarios might be will help you to determine whether you want to go the route of hybrid publishing or self-publishing. You might also gather various bids for services across both of these publishing options—and if you do, always make sure to get your hands on samples of the work of the company or person with whom you're thinking about collaborating.

Best Practices for Finding the Right Hybrid for You

With so many publishers self-identifying as hybrid these days, it's crucial to vet whatever publisher you're thinking of working with—and when you do, remember the IBPA checklist. Ask the hybrid publisher if they're aware of the checklist and whether they meet all the criteria. Ask them about their distribution and how that works. Do they do print runs? If so, where are those books stored? Make sure you also understand the ins and outs of the financials—what you'll be spending and how much you'll earn per book sold.

When you're considering working with a hybrid press, remember that there needs to be a vetting process, so they should review a submission and give you feedback. If that feedback is overly glowing or feels "salesy," take a minute to ground yourself before you proceed. Flattery is lovely, but flattery as a mechanism to get you to spend a bunch of money is called swindling.

Order the books of the hybrid publisher you're considering. Talk to authors who've previously published with that publisher. You could ask for a referral—but you don't have to. Cold-calling (or cold–direct messaging through social media) is perfectly acceptable. You can let the author know you're considering publishing with their publisher and ask them if it would be okay to ask some questions. Most hybrid-published authors are very happy to talk about their experience.

When connecting with a given publisher, you should be allowed access to a publisher, or at the very least to someone in a high position within the company—like an editorial director or an acquisitions manager. If you are connected to a sales person to finalize your deal, there's something wrong. If the person selling you a publishing package is an outsourced agency, there's something wrong. If you feel like you're being "up-sold"—which means pressured on the spot to add on services for a cost—there is something wrong.

When it comes to finding a hybrid publisher, you want to be alert and even just the tiniest bit cynical. Your book is an extension of yourself, for so many authors akin to a creative child they're birthing into the world. But it's exactly because of the value we place on our creativity and how vulnerable we can be around our hopes and expectations for our books that authors get taken advantage of. Make sure to spend time gathering information, talking to other authors, and trusting your gut when it comes to the person and/or company that you'll be entrusting with what may very well may be the most important creative work of your life.

You, Published Author

At the end of this entire journey through hybrid, should you choose to go this route, you will be a published author. The truth is that the success you have as an author lies in your hands. Very few people care who your publisher is; they care that the book reads well, looks beautiful, and is available for purchase wherever they buy books.

Once you're published, you must undertake the hard but rewarding work of continuing to promote your book. Part of the work of a hybrid-published author is to supplement the efforts of their publisher by visiting bookstores, especially local ones, to make sure the book is being carried. Building awareness for your book among industry professionals takes ongoing effort, and if you're going to spend the time, energy, and resources to be a hybrid-published author, I recommend carving out significant time in the six months following your book's release to spend time, time, and more time on your marketing and publicity efforts.

Traditional publishing has strong roots in elitism, and has culti-vated power through its acquisitions mechanism—the process of submitting to agents who represent you and then sell your book to a publisher for a giant advance. Most authors I know harbored a dream, at one time at least, to be published by one of the Big 5 publishers. Some have confessed to me their fantasies of the red-carpet treatment, allured by the possibility of becoming famous and selling tens of thousands of books. At some point in their journey, however, the reality of where the industry stands, currently, starts to set in. The recognition of how the Big Five actually work—the risk-adverse acquisitions, the tendency to lean in to already-famous authors or rising star-lets—can be disheartening, but also freeing.

I gave a TEDx talk a few years ago about another kind of power that authors themselves can cultivate, and that's green-lighting yourself and your work. The truth of the matter is that getting rejected by a traditional publisher has less to do with the quality of your book and everything to do with what you will quantifi-ably bring—or don't bring—to the table, according to their metrics. As I mentioned earlier, there are many reasons authors won't get traditional deals, but that there are so many things that have nothing to do with the quality of the work—not having a strong enough author platform, or following; being a debut author; starting the process at an advanced age; catering to too niche of an audience—are terrible reasons to put your own publishing dreams on hold.

Writers need books in order to build strong platforms; debut authors need to get published in order to establish a track record; older authors who are publishing the book they always wanted to write should be celebrated for their ambitions; an author who's written a book similar to something else that's been published should be encouraged by this news, as it means there's a readership for what they're writing; and if you know how to reach your readers, a niche audience can be a veritable gold mine.

Choosing to go the hybrid publishing route is a way to green-light your work with confidence. If you're publishing with a reputable hybrid, their reputation is on the line, too, so you will not face the kinds of newbie mistakes that will too often happen among self-published authors. Most importantly, once your book is in the world, you are a published author, and the question of how you got published and who published you will rarely come up, unless you choose for that conversation to be one you want to focus on. Publishing is a journey, and hybrid is an option for you if what it has to offer appeals to you. No matter your path, it's the confidence you show in your work as you market, talk about, and sell your book—not so much how the book got published—that will catapult you to success. Choosing the right hybrid house will be a key first step.

Top 10 Countdown

10. Read up on the publisher you're considering and make sure you're in alignment with their program—both in terms of the kind of book you're writing and with your own goals and values.

9. Make sure you can have a conversation with someone in a meaningful position at the publisher, and that you're not being passed off to a salesperson to close the deal.

8. Order the publisher's books and make sure they look and feel just like any other book on your shelf—that the quality is indistinguishable from traditionally published books.

7. Consider your budget and what costs you'll be putting into your book over what period of time so you go in with your eyes wide open, expectations set.

6. Do some information-gathering about the publishers you want to work with. Ask for materials they might be able to share with you and get familiar with what they publish.

5. Educate yourself about the industry by attending panels or looking up archived webinars about hybrid publishing so you understand its ins and outs.

4. Look up other hybrid published authors. Check out their websites, their online presence, and more and start to consider how you'll show up in the world as a published author.

3. Tend to or keep growing your author platform—meaning create or update your website, grow your social media, consider hiring someone to help you. Growing your audience is a necessary part of becoming an author, and it's never too early to start.

2. Sign up to become a member of the Independent Book Publishers Association and The Authors' Guild, two associations that offer so many resources and so much support to Indy authors.

1. Know when you're ready to green-light yourself, you'll feel it in your heart and in your gut, and once you do, you'll move forward with confidence as a future Indy author.

Meet Brooke Warner

Brooke Warner is publisher of She Writes Press and SparkPress, president of Warner Coaching Inc., and author of *Write On, Sisters!, Green-light Your Book, What's Your Book?,* and three books on memoir. Brooke is a TEDx speaker, weekly podcaster (of "Write-minded" with co-host Grant Faulkner of NaNoWriMo), and the former Executive Editor of Seal Press. She writes a regular column for *Publishers Weekly*.

www.brookewarner.com

www.shewritespress.com

www.writeyourmemoirinsixmonths.com

http://www.magicofmemoir.com

Working With Publishers
Grace Sammon

Your goal is clear. You want your book in print with readers, reviewers, and book clubs clamoring to get their hands on it. You have explored agents, traditional presses, hybrid presses, and author services firms. For purposes herein, we will refer to all these options as publishers. It feels like the really hard part of the bookwork is behind you. You've typed "the end," selected your publishing path, and now you "just" need to get this book out the door. This feels like you've already accomplished the hard part . . . writing the book . . . and you've moved onto the easy part, that is until you actually lock in a contract and begin your journey to the finish line of publishing.

This chapter is geared at helping you negotiate those next steps after the well-deserved deep breath and the celebratory "I am being published!" exclamation. The hard news upfront is that regardless of your path . . . whether you've successfully signed with an agent who has negotiated a publishing contract for your work or signed with an author services firm or anywhere in between . . . you still have a lot of work to do. Don't rush it. This is manageable. You've got this.

Working with a publisher is an acquired skill. I know. My first book was self-published, and by self-published, I mean I wrote it, formatted it, did the cover design, proudly drove over to the office supply store, had it spiral bound, and sold all the copies. In truth, it was a very lucrative venture and propelled me on a career as an educator and national keynote speaker. Also, it paved the way for me to be taken seriously as an author who could commit to the task of getting her work into the hands of readers. This is something that agents and publishers look for in their authors.

I've written both fiction and non-fiction. The process of having non-fiction published is wholly different than fiction. My second and third books were traditionally published with Corwin Press, a well-respected educational press. I had eleven publishers to choose from. My novel, *The Eves*, released from a hybrid press. And now, with this series of *Launch Pad* books, I am returning to a traditional press. As you will read throughout this book there are pros and cons to each journey. You will make more or less money and have more or less control of your final work with each option as well. What does not change is that you, the author, still ultimately have a large responsibility for the clarity, brilliance, and professionalism of your work. In this chapter, we are going to look at establishing a positive and effective working relationship with those who will be helping shape your final book.

It Starts with Expectations

In other chapters of this book, you're urged to look over in great detail any contract you enter into regarding your book. I, of course, echo that sentiment, but I'm going to suggest that even before that step you ask yourself the question of what it is you want from a publisher and what you expect from the process. Wrong expectations are the source of many of life's disappointments, and you don't need to set yourself up for frustration and disappointment at this stage in the writing process.

There are really two sets of expectations to be dealt with, mindset questions and business questions. I want to address both. The mindset questions are related to your emotional readiness to gear-up and bring your book to life. The business ones relate to how to make both the process and the outcome best work for you. The first mindset question is, are you ready for this to be a business? If the answer to that is no, then you have to decide if you want to get yourself ready or change course.

On the business side of things, you will want to have a host of questions ready for your potential publisher. These include how negotiable the contract is, what level of marketing is provided, how much control you have in the editorial and cover design process, what copyright and other rights do you maintain, what are you signing away, how are books distributed, whether to do a print run or print-on-demand, and how are royalties paid out. The answers to all of these differ from contract-to-contract, and understanding them at the outset will help you in managing the overall project.

On the mindset side of the house, how much time do you have to get this to press? There can be a three-year timeline to publication for some traditional presses, much shorter timelines for hybrid presses, and shorter still for author services firms. A professionally edited volume should be your ultimate goal. Going into the publishing process knowing that you will have multiple rounds of edits—developmental, copy, and line; as well as a proofread version of your book that will leave you bleary-eyed—will at least prepare you for the amount of time you are going to have to set aside to work on this process.

And, speaking of time, be clear on each of the deadlines for these benchmarks and your estimated publication date as early as possible. This is important both on an emotional level and a pragmatic one. Emotionally, you've worked hard, you want your book in the world! Pragmatically, you need to begin to lay out a marketing plan and timeline. Don't forget to ask about what technologies are used to move works toward publication. You may need to get a tutorial or brush up on your skills to work within the publisher's established protocols.

You will also want to consider asking to be introduced to your team at the publishing house. Depending on the path you have chosen you may have multiple people to work with at each editing stage and at the book layout and cover design stage. Knowing the players upfront can be a huge help. Asking your key point person at your publisher to lay out who the players are and their roles will help set the tone for success.

A key piece of managing expectations will be what are *you* really expected to do. The contract will lay some of this out but there is much that may be unclear, not by intent, but by the nature of the work of being an author today. I have colleagues who unexpectedly had to pay for additional editing services, for example. Still, others were left to design all of their promotional materials. I can't stress enough that your time is a valuable commodity in the publishing process and knowing expectations will help you budget that time wisely.

I've found that in a world where authors are involved in the publishing and promotion process of their books in unprecedented ways, it's easy to have what in the contracting business is called "scope creep." Scope creep is when suddenly you are doing more than you thought you were contracted to do. In all honesty, it works both ways—all of a sudden, your publisher has a great idea and has developed some new promotion for the book that requires work on both your parts. It's scope creep, but it's also a benefit to you and the publisher. What I want to caution you about here is taking on more than you intended, more than the contract asks of you. Let me be clear, and I'll address this in a bit below, I am not saying don't allow scope creep, just be aware that at this stage anything that takes you away from building a marketing plan for your work-in-progress or keeps you from you writing your next work is a dangerous aside to your ultimate goal of being successfully published.

Full disclosure here, I'll give the example of writing and publishing this *Launch Pad* series. When I first conceived of the series I went to Emma Dhesi, an author and book coach to be my co-author on book one, our book on writing. I went to Mary Helen Sheriff, who you will meet in book three, for our book on marketing. Mary is an author and also runs a business helping authors successfully market their books without losing their minds. We then approached Stephanie Larkin, CEO of Red Penguin Books out of New York, to publish our books. We successfully inked a deal with Red Penguin, a firm with over 14 years of experience. We entrusted Red Penguin with the contributing author contacts and required releases, editorial process, cover design, web development, promotional materials, and all aspects of publishing. Stephanie became my co-lead on this volume. She and Red Penguin did what was contracted and did it well. Then, enter three type-A and, dare I say, skilled series team leaders in the shapes of Emma, Mary, and me. Let me tell you what happened. Scope creep.

The three of us, admittedly me more than the others, put our hands in the publishing pie. Emma, Mary, and I had a huge publishing learning curve and a style of business established over years in our own companies. We knew a lot of publishers, but little about publishing. Yet, we questioned and developed and redeveloped materials. We each went down the "Canva" rabbit hole of designing social media posts and videos. This demanded a lot of us and a great deal of patience from Stephanie. At one point we even suggested that we renegotiate the already-signed contract! Did I mention patience is important?

The result is a three-book series of which we are collectively quite proud. Each of us, including Stephanie, learned a lot. We all became smarter and better at our craft in the process. However, I am sure each of us, in hindsight, would agree that some of the work was redundant and kept us from being focused on other areas of our work that needed attention, brought in revenue, or fed our author souls.

The last external piece of expectations is to make sure you understand how "launch day" will roll out. Of course, you are hoping for great reviews, well-positioned interviews, a launch party, and the like . . . those types of events you'll learn more about in book three on marketing. For now, make sure you understand the logistics of your launch. How does your book get released? On what platforms and in what formats? How will it be advertised? Will there be any publicity support? How and when do you get author copies and advanced reader copies? What "keywords" are being used to attract readers? These are just a few critical questions that need to be answered early to set you up for success and the all-important planning you need to be looking ahead toward.

Key to any thinking around expectations should be what do you expect from yourself. Let's be honest, not all of us have the metal to get through the publishing process, at least not without several head-banging sessions of frustration and self-questioning. How hands-on do you need to be and can you be are also critical questions. It all goes back to the goal. If your goal is to get this book out, trust the people you are working with, and let them do their job. Be a partner in the process. Hire, if you can, anyone you need to support you to fill in your blank skill sets.

It's About Relationships

My generation (ok, I am old) knows that a lot is accomplished by practicing the common niceties, small gestures, generosity of spirit, and attention to detail. These are the cornerstones for establishing positive working relationships with people, and you are going to want to work at this as you head down the potentially bumpy path to publishing. Take the time to get to know the people who are going to be working at getting your book into print, not just what their role is but who they are. Remembering that we are all people first . . . with lives outside of publishing, family obligations, health issues, children, and the like . . . will come in handy when you are wondering why it's two o'clock on a Sunday afternoon and your copy editor hasn't gotten back to you since you sent that last email at 2:00 AM.

I've already mentioned the complexities of getting these *Launch Pad* volumes in your hands. There could have been, okay, there were, moments where I doubted that I had it in me to publish the series. Keep in mind, this is my sixth book. I thought I had this publishing thing down pat. Clearly, I'm still learning. Which is a very good thing. What sustained Emma, Mary, Stephanie, and me was that the four of us on the *Launch Pad* publishing team kept in mind that we were people first. During the publishing process, we had family deaths and births, missing children, gymnastic meets, and trips to wineries. Life goes on, and it should. Books happen.

Being published is a long-haul game. Depending on your press, you may grow resentful of unexpected fees or an unforeseen need to, for example, do more editing. It may seem unfair when you are asked to read for the fourth time a manuscript you are now so close to you actually can't see the forest for the trees. Keeping an understanding of the importance of relationships at the center of your work will help. This will also help you when

you are just exhausted and think maybe you want to walk away–
which may not happen, but could.

This brings me to your relationship with you. Yes, this is outside
of the scope of this chapter (oh no, scope creep), but this entire
Launch Pad series is about supporting you as a writer who wants
to be published and who will then masterfully market your
book. Be gentle with you. I always describe writing as the most
naked thing I do. Putting words out there for others to comment
on, reshape, and reimagine is all part of the publishing process,
and it can be one that causes lots of self-questioning, late-night
and early-morning edit sessions, and a fair amount of soul-
searching. Take time to make sure you are taking time to eat
well, stay hydrated, and have a comfortable chair, good lighting,
and creature comforts that will sustain you through this work. In
book one, we talk about the importance of writing communities.
Then in book three, we talk about the importance of networking. Lean into these resources to sustain you while you are
working at the publishing stage.

Keep Writing

The best advice I can give you at this stage, and I am confident
that your publisher will agree, is to keep writing. You may have
had the "luxury" of taking years to write your current book but
your publisher and your readers will want another book in their
hands shortly. Agents and publishers are most interested in
authors that are going to continue to produce books. Readers,
especially today in the world of social media, want to engage
with you as an author, and they are waiting for your next book.
The truth is subsequent books will sell your current book and so
on. Besides, you are a writer. Writers write. Taking time to focus
on your next manuscript will feed your soul and keep you
focused. While we need to learn the ins and outs of publishing

in a way that no previous generation of authors has had to, we are at our core, writers.

Be Flexible—You Are Almost There

You've already worked through multiple rounds of edits. If you are lucky, you have had some influence on your cover design. You love it! You can already imagine the book on bookshelves! Then comes the email with just one more request from the publisher. This happened to me with my third book. I was traveling 200 days a year and honestly, I am not sure how I had time to even write *Battling the Hamster Wheel: Strategies for High School Improvement*. I needed this book done and out the door. Then, the publisher came back and said that the jury team felt the book really needed a study guide. A study guide? Seriously? I had zero idea how to create one, nor did I understand why one would be important. The jury team was right, however, the fact that I took the time to create a useful tool for educators made the book more sellable. More sales; more requests from school systems to hire my services to facilitate their study; which in turn turned into more revenue for me for national speaker fees. Creating the guide also paid off years later when I wrote my novel, *The Eves*. After the study guide experience, I was able to anticipate that an add-on in the shape of a complete Book Club Kit with questions, playlists, recipes, and more would enhance the sale of the book and position me for book clubs and community speaking engagements. The lesson here is even though you have typed "the end," anticipate and start working on elements that will enhance the quality of your book. It's worth discussing such a venture early on with your publisher.

Lastly, trust the process. Writers write. Let publishers publish. In an ideal world, your publishing team is in love with you and your work. In the real world, they want to sell books and run an effective business. In the real world, you want to sell books—this book and the next. When you sign that contract, you are entrusting yourself and your work to your publisher's skill set. Sure, you need to be vigilant, but trust the process. Enjoy the process. You are almost there!

Top 10 Countdown to Working with Publishers

Throughout this book, you will read multiple points of view about the path to publishing. Regardless of the path you choose . . . or chooses you . . . you will have to dive in, roll up your sleeves, and do more work than you anticipated. Keep your eye on the goal of getting your manuscript into the hands of readers. Publishers, their contracts, their staffs, and expectations are as varied as genres. Publishers want your book to succeed. To a large extent, you will still be responsible for putting the best book forward. Establishing a positive, collaborative, and time-sensitive working relationship will be key to that success.

10. Know your goal in getting published. Demonstrate that you are an author who is professional and can deliver and sustain your work as a serious writer. Target your search for a path to publishing based on your goal.

9. Learn as much as you can about the publisher or author services firm with whom you are signing.

8. Go beyond the contract and make sure you understand their expectations of you and make sure you are clear on what you can expect from them.

7. Be prepared. It's going to be way more work at this stage than you expected.

6. Work to establish a positive working relationship with your various editors, designers, etc.

5. Be patient. The path to publishing is not for the faint of heart or the hasty. You've got this.

4. Be working on your next book the entire time your current book is at the pre-launch/publishing stage. You will want another book ready as soon as possible.

3. Be flexible. You may think you are "done," but last-minute revisions, like the addition of a study guide or a book club package, can make all the difference in the book's success and yours.

2. Be open. The publisher wants your book to succeed and may see a path to that success that you do not see.

1. Enjoy the journey! You are about to be in print!

Meet Grace Sammon

Grace Sammon is recognized in "Who's Who in Education" and "Who's Who in Literature." She utilized skills built up over decades to re-invent herself with her award-winning fourth book and debut novel, *The Eves*. She is the brainchild behind the Launch Pad radio show and the three-book series on writing, publishing, and marketing your book. Grace also hosts The Storytellers on Authors on the Air Global Radio Network. Always committed to creative collaborations, Grace is the founder of Author Talk Network; a member of the Women's Fiction Writers' Association (WFWA) and the Women's National Book Association (WNBA). She is the Director of Membership for one of the fastest-growing reader/writer online communities "Bookish Road Trip." She currently lives on Florida's west coast with her husband and a small herd of imaginary llamas.

Find out more about Grace and her work at:

Website: www.GraceSammon.Net
Facebook: https://www.facebook.com/GraceSammonWrites/
Instagram: https://www.instagram.com/GraceSammonWrites/

Working With an Illustrator
Cydney Bittner

It's very important for any author who will be working directly with an illustrator to familiarize themself, on however basic a level, with different types of illustration. Having even a highly limited vocabulary to talk about your vision will be much more useful for communicating with your illustrator than having no vocabulary at all.

The most essential thing to familiarize yourself with is different media. The common media in illustration, especially in children's illustration, are watercolor, pencil, colored pencil, ink, and collage. Watercolor is one of, if not the most popular mediums used in illustration. It is incredibly versatile, as it can be used for smooth, polished, detailed work, or for loose, more abstract work. Watercolor can also easily be paired with other media, especially colored pencils or ink. The major benefit of colored pencils is that they can provide an extra sense of texture in an illustration, especially when used on top of smoothly-painted watercolor. They are absolutely beautiful on their own, as well. Regular graphite pencil illustration is likely going to be your best bet for any project that will be printed in black and white. It can be used to create drawings of excellent depth, contrast, and texture. Ink can be used on its own, especially for a black-and-white or simply monochromatic project. Ink can also be used to create clean, graphic outlines or to add depth and texture to other media, especially watercolor. Collage is great for creating highly textured, very vibrant, almost three-dimensional illustrations. Any and all of these media can be combined in any fashion.

Artists also frequently utilize digital art programs—the most popular being Adobe Photoshop, Adobe Illustrator, and Procreate—either on their own or in conjunction with traditional media. These programs have a massive variety of digital "brushes" that can imitate virtually any traditional media. The major perk to entirely digital illustration or simply using digital drawing programs to enhance a traditionally-made illustration is that it makes for uniquely clean, smooth lines, etc., and will translate perfectly to print. Your illustrator will likely have a preferred medium that he or she likes to work with, but will also likely be open to exploring different options. I encourage all authors who are working in tandem with illustrators to look at plenty of examples of different illustrations and really get a feel for what will best suit their stories.

The relationship between an author and illustrator is key to quality work. Here are some tips for a successful collaboration:

Treat Illustrators less like Picasso and more like your colleagues.

This is a slightly tongue-in-cheek piece of advice, but still good to remember! Many folks who have never worked with an illustrator, and maybe never even met an artist before, tend to stereotype creative people as flaky, quirky, wild-haired free spirits. Sure, there are artists out there who probably check the classic Picasso-Dali-Van Gogh-crazy-painter box, but odds are your illustrator is not going to be That Person. Illustration is a much more commercial, even a corporate-style enterprise, than painting. Illustrators attend meetings, sign contracts, network, negotiate, and talk to agents and accountants, and sometimes lawyers. If you're nervous about or unsure what to expect from working with an artist for the first time, it may be helpful to think of your illustrator more like a business person who happens to do art. We're just as sane and ordinary as anyone else—for whatever that's worth!

Understand that not all illustrators have worked directly with an author before.

Situations in which the author and illustrator of a book are working in direct communication/collaboration with one another are beautiful opportunities; the author gets to feel secure in knowing their book baby is being well cared for, and the illustrator gets to feel the author's joy and gratification in seeing their dream be realized step-by-step. However, it's important to bear in mind that this is not always the case—in fact, it's actually rare. More often than not, an illustrator is answerable to a publishing company's art director/design team, and the author doesn't have any contact with the illustrator at all. You, as the author, might want to bear this in mind, as many illustrators are used to working with other artistically-minded folks, and working with an author may be as much of an adjustment for them as working with an illustrator is for you.

Respect that illustrators are not book critics, editors, or publishers.

We are working with you to make this book everything you want it to be and more, but remember, many of us are not writers or editors, so please don't ask for criticism of the text. I have had several authors ask me such questions as "What do you think of __ part of the book?" or "What age demographic would you recommend for this book?" Not only is it not the illustrator's job to answer such questions, but these are also things that most likely should have been worked out before the illustrator even starts their work.

Appreciate that each artist is their own unique person.

You may be very fond of the work of a particular illustrator long past, or perhaps a contemporary illustrator that you just didn't happen to get to work with. While it helps to have a frame of reference for the style you want, remember that each artist is their own person; do NOT ask for your illustrator to outright copy the style of another illustrator. The artwork can be inspired by other, pre-existing content, but artistic integrity is important and should not be compromised.

Be open-minded.

You may have a distinct vision in mind for your book before even consulting with an illustrator. That's great, and your illustrator will be very appreciative to have as much direction and clarity as you can provide. However, as we discussed earlier, your illustrator is a unique person with their own ideas and will likely have a vision of their own. That being said, a book is a collaborative effort, and both parties should be open to different ideas, open to compromise, and open to the joys of artistic exploration!

Beware of the word "cartoon."

I cannot tell you how many times this word has come up while working with authors. The word "cartoon" is a problem for a multitude of reasons, and an author should strike it from their vocabulary. To begin with, "cartoon" is a very broad term; it simply means a drawing done in an unrealistic or semi-realistic manner and has also come to refer to animations. Think about the comics section of a newspaper. Those are all cartoons, but you wouldn't say they all look the same, would you? Go even further and think about all the animated movies and television shows you've ever seen. All cartoons. All vastly different. See the issue? When an author says he or she "doesn't want cartoons," he/she is not saying much.

Another problem occurs specifically when an author expresses distaste for "cartoons." He/she rarely realizes that the word can virtually encapsulate everything that isn't realism. Many authors of children's picture books who claim to not want cartoons do not want realism, either, but simply do not have the vocabulary to describe what it is they do want.

Authors, no one expects you to have a well-cultivated vocabulary and understanding of art, but please try to avoid the word cartoon as best as you can, and if you can't, try to list the cartoons in popular media that you do or don't like. The more specific you can get, the better we can visualize what it is you want.

Instead of "great minds think alike," think "great minds may reach the same conclusion, but often arrive there differently."

If an author and illustrator are well-matched, ideally, their respective visions will align beautifully. However, they are not the same person. An author is likely to think and express themself better in words and writing. Many artists are more visual thinkers and may struggle with verbally communicating all of their ideas. To put this in context: say an author and illustrator are trying to figure out what should be depicted on a specific spread. An author might believe that the text on the page is enough guidance, as words are enough to tell a story. The illustrator, on the other hand, is likely going to visualize dozens of possible compositions in his/her mind. The author may be unprepared to compare multiple variations of the same scene, simply because he/she doesn't think that way and never realized there were so many ways to depict the same event. The illustrator may be unprepared to explain his/her methodology, thought processes, etc. Be mindful of and patient with one another's different, beautiful brains. That being said…

Communicate, communicate, COMMUNICATE.

As we have already established, both author and illustrator are unique individuals. They may have different visions, different ways of thinking, and different ways of communicating. That means you both—in many ways, the author most of all—are going to have to do your best to be very, very clear with one another. If you're struggling to interpret storyboards, say so, and ask questions! If you're not a fan of a proposed illustration, explain why not, and be as specific as possible. Illustrators want to provide the best results possible, but we need clear, constructive feedback to do so!

Come prepared, but don't be scared!

Think of this as an extension of the advice I provided for the "cartoon" dilemma. Authors are typically not used to thinking in the visual and typically do not have much knowledge of different art/illustration styles or even art media. That's okay! Don't be intimidated by your illustrator's knowledge and experience, and do not think they will be upset with you for not knowing all the ins and outs of illustration. Illustrators do not expect authors to be well-versed in that department. One thing you can do to make the collaborative process go more smoothly for everyone is research! Not technical vocabulary or anything like that, just some examples of books, illustrations, artists, etc. that fit the tone and style you'd like the book to have. If you can, try to make a mood board–if you have Pinterest, even better! Gather as many relevant references as you can. This is tremendous in helping the artist get as close to your vision as possible!

Realize that illustration takes time and energy.

One of the most important pieces of advice I can provide is to remember that the artistic process is a time- and energy-consuming process. Illustrators expect to make revisions, to reimagine a concept if it isn't working out, and so forth, but be reasonable. Many illustrators will limit the number of revisions, usually to a final illustration, that they will do before expecting additional compensation. Furthermore, while some illustrators will agree to a flat fee for the project, many illustrators charge by time. Asking for 12 different variations of a finished spread is not only impractical for the artist, but it is also impractical for the overall budget and timeline of the project. Be realistic; be respectful. Illustrators are passionate about their jobs, but at the end of the day, it's still *work* and should be treated as such by all parties involved.

Top 10 Countdown to Working with an Illustrator

10. Treat illustrators less like Picasso and more like your colleagues.

9. Understand that not all illustrators have worked directly with an author before.

8. Respect that illustrators are not book critics, editors, or publishers.

7. Appreciate each artist as a unique person.

6. Be open-minded.

5. Beware of the word "cartoon."

4. Instead of "great minds think alike," think "great minds may reach the same conclusion but often arrive there differently."

3. Communicate, communicate, COMMUNICATE.

2. Come prepared, but don't be scared!

1. Realize that illustration takes time and energy.

Meet Cydney Bittner

Cydney Bittner is a children's and fantasy illustrator based in Bucks County, Pennsylvania. She received a B.A. in Studio Art and Illustration & Animation from Marymount Manhattan College in 2021. Her illustration credits include *Libby the Ladybug Learns Helpfulness* by Carly Furino, *George the Alligator Finds a Home* by Margaret Sansom, *The 7 Days: A Classic Nursery Rhyme Made New* by Deborah Burns, and *Bella the Buck-Toothed Ballerina* by Amanda Montoni. When she's not illustrating books or painting fantasy scenes, Cydney also works as an art instructor. In her experience teaching, she has seen firsthand the importance of imagination; she strives to create art that nurtures that critical part of the human psyche.

website: cydneybittner.myportfolio.com

instagram: @cydneybittnerart

Wide or Kindle Unlimited

D. C. Gomez

Whether you are an aspiring author or a seasoned vet, you have probably heard the debate going around about the best way to publish the eBook version of your manuscript—through Amazon's Kindle Unlimited (KU) or "going wide" or just "wide," meaning your book is available beyond the Amazon platform. Maybe you are like me, contemplating the pros and cons of each marketing system. The reality can be confusing because there is no one-size-fits-all approach to publishing or to being an author. No one approach to publishing will make sense for your career. What works for one successful author might be the downfall of another. What works for one book may not work for another. Don't worry, my dear author, this is perfectly normal. (And yes, you are an author. If you are writing, creating stories, but you haven't published your first book, you are still an author. Just one working on becoming a published author.)

The world of publishing and writing comes with many paths and lots of options. Our goal as authors is to find the one that makes sense to us and is authentic to our beliefs and ideals. Finding the right one can take time, and unfortunately sometimes too much money. But if you are reading this book, you are way ahead of the curve. You are learning from others and taking the things that fit you to make it your own. So, let's jump right into this debate.

My goal is not to tell you which one to pick but to give you the options in order for you to make the best decision. If you are *traditionally published*, this chapter might be harder to implement than if you are an Indy author, or even going with a small press. The major publishing companies will make this distribution decision for you and find the best way to market your book. On average, most publishers will release a book wide and work on getting it in as many hands as possible.

For an Indy author, as well as many small presses, this is a huge decision—do I go wide or Amazon/KU-exclusive? Before going too far here, let's define these terms. When we are referring to wide, we are talking about specifically releasing your eBooks to all major distribution companies (Kindle, Apple Books, Barnes and Noble, Kobo, you name it) all at once. Please note, we are talking about Kindle here, just not the exclusive-only program. An exclusive agreement is one where your eBook is only available with one major distributor at a time. The most well-known one is Amazon's Kindle Unlimited Program. While others have their own exclusive program, for this chapter, we are going to focus on KU only. However, the rules are pretty similar for the others.

I noticed recently that most authors don't realize we are only talking about the eBook here. This means you can be exclusive in KU for your eBook and at the same time have your print book wide with anyone else you choose. (If you are publishing through Kindle and opt into having your paperback released through their network, they will distribute to everyone, including Barnes and Nobles and even Kobo. Just something to keep in mind.)

Going Wide!

What are the pros and cons of being a wide author? This might sound a little mushy, but you first have to decide what level of risk you can handle. It's perfectly okay to be emotional about this. Dealing with risk normally involves a lot of feelings. If you have ever been to a financial advisor to discuss investing in the stock market, this is the same type of question. How comfortable are you with taking risks? There is no right or wrong answer here, dear author. You just have to take a close look at how you handle stress and how you feel about having your eggs all in one basket.

Most wide authors are trying to avoid having all their income solely dependent on one store. Going wide means you have more income revenue streams and can advertise on other platforms at your own pace. This means if one store takes your book off their "virtual" shelves, you still have other sources of income.

One negative to being a wide author is the fact that you have to manage multiple distribution locations. You can use a third-source distributor (like Draft2Digital or D2D) to distribute your books to all locations all at once or do it yourself individually. There are options out there. The trick is to remember building a wide readership takes time. The advertisement that works for one platform does not necessarily translate to others. Distributors like Apple, Barnes and Noble, and even Kobo don't have the same algorithm to send readers to your books as easily as Amazon.

Should I be exclusive?

What exactly is KU? The easiest way to think about it is as a digital library. For a monthly membership of $9.99 (at least at the printing of this book), readers can read as many books as they like that are part of the KU program. Readers are allowed to have up to 10 books in their carts at any given time. But like any library program, you can turn one in and get another one. For avid readers, this is the holy grail. With eBooks costing anywhere from $2.99 and up, readers might not have the funds to purchase every book they would like to read.

Authors get paid by the pages read. Unfortunately, like everything Amazon does, there is no published formula for how much we get paid per page. You can check the number of pages read every day in your Kindle dashboard (as well as your number of books sold and even returned). The amount of money paid to the author varies from month to month. On average, most authors estimate their pages get paid roughly $.0044 (but nobody is truly 100% sure). This means a 300-page book might earn you about $1.32 per reader. If you sold the same book for $2.99 and received the 70% return, you would get $2.09. You would make more money selling an eBook directly than going to KU. So why do it?

KU has its own organic fan base. Their readership is voracious and consumes books faster than anything else. Fans can easily feature your book on Amazon's recommendation list based on that genre and make recommendations to a warm reader looking for similar books. And because they have so many readers, your pages read can add up quickly. Also, as part of the KU program, Amazon lets you run eBook deals. You can advertise your books for $.99 for up to seven days while keeping your 70% royalty. Granted 70% after distribution fees for a $.99 book is not a lot of money, but if you sell a lot, it's a great way to get new readers who are not in KU.

Another prominent part of KU is their KU campaign, where you can put your book for FREE for seven days. This might not seem like a big deal at first, but Amazon does not let you have free books on their sites. The only way to pull that off (besides the KU deals) is to have your book wide on the other major platforms (recommend at least two) for free. Once that happens, you can ask Amazon to price-match the book. This can be fairly long and tedious, but worth it if you are looking for a reader's magnet.

With the KU free deals, the book is free for a period. You just have to pick your days, and Amazon does the rest. Once the time has expired, the book goes back to its regular price. Remember, Amazon is all about making money. They are not very concerned about our careers; that is our job.

KU has one of the largest exclusive programs out there for authors. Without a doubt, the creation of Kindle books is the reason many of us can publish our books without fighting the old publishing gatekeepers. When you enter into a KU agreement, it is considered a "membership" program between you as the author and Amazon as the distributor, but it also comes with some issues.

Amazon can take an author's account down for "violating" their KU policy. If you are not familiar with this, let's break it down. If you decide to have your eBook in KU, this means for ninety days your eBook cannot be available in any store or website (including your own) for sale or even free. They allow 10% of the manuscript to be used in other sources without any penalties but no more. KU reserves the rights to the sale of this product. As an author, you can have your membership automatically renew or terminate the contract after ninety days. This doesn't sound too bad. But if your book is distributed without your permission (i.e. pirated), and Amazon finds out, they will terminate your contract and, on most occasions, cancel your account.

Please be aware, eBooks are pirated all the time. One of the most common ways books are pirated is by using unvetted ARCs (Advance Reader Copy). This is when you send your eBook (usually prior to distribution) to readers for them to read/review in an effort to gain feedback and many times "reviews" on a platform. It's not always the case, but we have seen cases of these readers admitting to joining an author platform just to gain access to a book and pirating it. I have been a victim of this myself. I would recommend taking some time to vet your street team prior to sending your books out to anyone.

This is the reality many authors fear, and one that many readers witnessed this past year. Through no fault of the author, their books were being sold on pirates' sites. Amazon took drastic actions (or typical Amazon actions) and punished the author. But before I scare everyone away, many KU authors have taken proactive actions to monitor their books and potential pirate sites. It just means a lot more work for the author.

If you are wondering why would an author put their eggs in this one basket, the answer is simple. Amazon owns 85% of the book market. Their Kindle Unlimited bonus program gives back to authors 40 million dollars annually. Before you get really excited, I might need to explain that you need over 100,000 pages read each month (usually closer to half a million) to qualify for the bonus. That's right in the KU world you get paid by the number of pages read. Readers don't even need to read your whole book in order for you to benefit from the KU membership. The bonuses are real and happen each month.

Myths Going Around

Before we go any further, I want to dispel a few myths that I have encountered in my career.

> Myth #1: *You can start your career in KU and then go wide. Those readers will follow you and buy your eBooks at full price.* Unfortunately, this is not always the case, my friend. KU readers are and will be KU readers. Very few of them are jumping out to buy your eBook. Many of my friends tried this transition and have found that their KU readers rarely

follow them out. If anything, many were angry that the author was not in the program anymore. If you are planning to be a wide author, focus your effort on building your readership wide from the beginning. If you switch mid-way, most likely you will see a drop in revenue as readers work on your transition.

Myth #2: *You can't make a lot of money going wide.* This is definitely not true. I know plenty of authors whose entire collections are wide. It took them longer to build a readership than many KU-only authors. They spend a lot more time cultivating their fans and providing consistent work. In turn, they have seen their readers follow them from one series to another.

Now, what to do?

The beautiful thing is you have options. I'm a huge believer that everything doesn't have to be black and white. Many of my friends and readers are in KU. I'm very conscious of the cost of purchasing books. In the beginning, many of my readers felt bad that they couldn't purchase my books and could only read KU. It took me some time to educate them on how authors make money on KU. Once they realized authors were still making money from pages being read, they were thrilled and took advantage of their perks.

For me, one size doesn't fit all. I'm a bit too risk-phobic to trust any one organization with my livelihood (even Amazon and I'm an Amazon junkie). I currently have one full urban fantasy series in KU (five novels). The rest of my books are already wide or in transition to going wide.

One technique that I practice that has worked really well for me is releasing my books first in KU for 90-180 days. Depending on the genre, I then transition them wide. This process gave my KU readers an opportunity to get the book. Then, switching out, it allowed me to sell the book directly and use them as part of my other marketing campaigns (i.e. my new Kickstarter campaign). It's a compromise of both systems, instead of being all or nothing.

This approach doesn't work for everyone. Some of my friends have all their books in KU. It gives them a natural algorithm to target and a lot fewer headaches since they aren't managing multiple platforms. Others have gone directly wide and not looked back.

Regardless of which platform you decide to use, read their contracts before joining. Make sure you are meeting the requirements for distribution. Analyze how long the contracts are for and how much you will be getting. Take advantage of any promotion programs they have and work on maximizing their specific algorithm.

Once you decide to publish your book, you become a small business owner. Treat this part of your career as a business. Take your time researching the distribution programs available to you. If you don't have time to load your book individually to every site, use a third party. If you don't want to manage multiple platforms and are comfortable with your books being only in one area, then go exclusive. Remember, there is no right or wrong answer here (regardless of what anyone says). You are in charge of this journey, and if you decide to change your mind and switch it up, do it!

At the end of the day, this is your journey. Have a blast with it. Make the most of your writing career and your business. As the famous quote says, you are the master of your boat! Go forth, my dear author friend, publish that book!

Top 10 Countdown – Considerations Before Committing to a Distributing Platform

10. Determine your comfort level for risk. Know yourself and your own level of comfort when it comes to having all your income come from one location or multiple is crucial.

9. Assess how much time you have available for uploading-updating your books on multiple platforms. This is something we normally do not think about. However, it does take time to learn each system and keep your books updated.

8. If considering wide, research the options between using a third party and doing it all yourself. This goes back to your time commitment. Can you handle managing three to five different platforms or just one?

7. If considering exclusive distribution, review the time requirement each platform mandates for their program. This part can take time in the beginning but can save many headaches later on. Some of the major platforms to start with are Amazon's Kindle program, Barnes and Noble, KOBO, Draft2Digital, and IngramSpark.

6. If considering exclusive, research if other major venues like Barnes and Noble or even Apple will give you a higher royalty than Amazon. While KU is the biggest platform for eBooks, it is not the only one. Not everyone wants to play in Amazon. You do have options.

5. If you would like your books available to libraries, a third-party distributor like Draft2Digital is a great option to research.

4. Remember, you can have your eBook exclusive in one platform, while your print books are wide. Your print books and eBooks are separate entities when it comes to publishing. Make sure to take advantage of this and maximizes your options.

3. Ask for feedback from authors in your genre. While the publishing world is very unique genre-to-genre, researching what is working in the market can be very beneficial to making an informed decision.

2. Don't be afraid to experiment with options. Even if you decided to go exclusively with one platform, you can change your mind and try something different later. See what works for you.

1. Give yourself time to explore all your options. Just do not fall into "analysis paralysis." This means, at some point you just need to make a decision.

Meet D. C. Gomez

D. C. Gomez is an award-winning USA Today Bestselling Author, Podcaster, motivational speaker, and coach. Born in the Dominican Republic, she grew up in Salem, Massachusetts. D. C. studied film and television at New York University. After college, she joined the US Army and proudly served for four years.

D. C. has a master's degree in Science Administration from Central Michigan University, as well as a masters in Adult Education from Texas A&M-Texarkana University. She is a certified John Maxwell Team speaker and coach, as well as a certified meditation instructor from the Chopra Center.

One of D. C.'s passions is helping those around her overcome their self-limiting beliefs. She writes non-fiction as well as fiction books, ranging from Urban Fantasy to Children's Books.

To learn more about her books and her passion, you can find her at:

Website: www.dcgomez-author.com

The Mystery of Self-Publishing
Wilnona Marie

The End!

Uh, no. This is the beginning, but the beginning of what? Well, that is up to you. In other chapters, the beginning of the traditional and hybrid publishing journey is given attention. Here we will discuss self-publishing. Yes, this is the publishing option available to everyone, but it still remains a mystery to many new writers. Like a mystery, let's find out if the culprit "self-publishing" is worth pursuing for you.

Enter the mystery of self-publishing.

Cryptic notes encircle the author like a crescent moon, somewhere there is the truth. Sifting through the information is a daunting task, and it isn't one that the author is looking forward to. This case has trudged on beyond any expected due date.

In the corner, her faux wood desk sags in the middle as a result of queries into the publishing and retaining of an agent, all with no results. Research had gone into each selection before the lead was pursued. Although the writer knows she is spectacular at her skill set, doubts were making inroads. The moisture of "what ifs" was trickling down those inroads, filling her mind with the scent of mildewed ideas and regurgitated notions. Something would have to be done, and it had to be soon. If not, that crescent moon will dissolve into the daylight of failure for all to see.

Pressure builds as those closest to the author become antsy about the potential end of the case. It is said that stress causes people to do crazy things. But in this case, it isn't a disease of the mind or a desperate act, the next move will be a deliberate blow, one of precision. Renewed determination fills the wordsmith from toenail to hair follicle. There is an answer out there, and the author is going to find it this night.

The writer thinks. With digits flying across the keyboard, keys clacking in a whirring rhythm, the author into the night escapes. The motions on the keys in front of them bring forth a name. The case heads in another direction. After exhausting names and their company connections, the red herring that previously hung on the wall looks more and more like a clue. The scribe finds the card in a pile for randomly housed things, picks it up, and feels a spark of possibility grow into a flame.

"IngramSpark," softly escapes her lips.

She begins to type with one hand. A bolt of nervous energy/fear electrifies her as she waits for the page to load. The would-be published author recalls horror tales of self-publishing and fears the shadowy folk who lie in these alleys. Will they lunge out with scams in their hand ready to puncture the author's dreams? Is there a possibility of being stolen away into the sorrow of not understanding the process and drowning her own dreams in this new world of literary discoveries? A quick scroll through the website offers up nuggets of information about the elusive culprit. "Publishing" could be caught by doing it yourself! The thoughts permeates the penman's frontal cortex and starts to ruminate. All this time the prey could have been ensnared by the writer's own hand. How could this be?

Clues come forthwith as the web searches create deluges of information. There is also hybrid publishing, a mix of traditional and self-publishing. Prices are attached to each package, promising a published book at the end. Reputable sites like Salt Water Media, a selective hybrid press where the writer pays a set fee for the publisher to do the work of publishing the book, emerge. Self-publishing is no longer looked at as if the author went to the local office supply company to print their book, the writer noticed. There are so many good Indy and hybrid presses that have all the services and menu options to help with the whole process. She Writes Press is an award-winning press and is represented by all the standards set forth by the Independent Book Publishers Association (IBP). Their authors have been featured on the *Today* show, in *The Atlantic* magazine, and in *People* magazine.

As impressive as this news is, the writer knows there is more exploration in this DIY world to be done. Upon further investigation in the dark of their living room, the scribe chooses to flatfoot it alone on the unknown streets of self-publishing. As the to-be-published author gathers her wits about her and sets foot on this path, so many questions are left unanswered by search engines. Yet the determination for publication and the scattered crescent moon of rejection letters strewn about the floor and desk move the story scribbler forward. There is much to investigate, discover, and decide upon before daybreak.

The first suspect is Amazon, the book business that rules supreme nowadays. Kindle Direct Publishing (KDP) is the platform she studied. The book needs a title, a manuscript, and an International Standard Book Number (ISBN) for uniquely identifying books or an Amazon Standard Identification Number (AISN). The identification code is a string of numbers that earmarks and codifies a book. Information such as title, author, type of book, physical properties, and location of the publisher are included in your ISBN/AISN, and the number is different for the print book, eBook, or audiobook. A little piece of every book's ISBN offers a solution to the mystery of publishing. How many times had she seen a barcode and a string of numbers and thought of nothing more than the price?

The book cover could be created within KDP. Distribution of the paperback could be done by KDP. This is a one-stop shop, but is it all it's cracked up to be? Was there a dark side to the bright promises of publication?

Upon arrival at the other powerhouses' doors, the scribe learns so much more from each company's website. The storyteller feels some confidence in the information gathered from the other sources. Although it is a close call because she almost jumped before she was ready, she had discerned the problems. It seems in her haste to get to publication, she had overlooked a few clues. Within the halls of YouTube, she found the tools needed to better navigate in order to find the truth.

There is more to uncover. There are free ISBNs offered, ASINs, and ISBN bundles. Free ISBNs provided by the platform can only be used by the platform which offered the ISBN. They cannot be transferred to another publisher. Beating the streets of self-publishing and trying to close in on the perp that was getting away leaves the writer befuddled.

The corner light flickering a pattern similar to morse code for help prompts the question of using book consultants to help guide the way. If not for them, a safe silo is the KDP discussion page or becoming part of the many Indy neighborhoods in social media.

To stay on the straight and narrow in a place shrouded in secrecy, there is no greater light than the written word. Turning once more to the clues that had guided her to these streets, the writer reviewed what she has learned already. She reviews what brought her to these self-navigated streets and works backward toward her manuscript. The still elusive prey is nabbing a publishing path. That starts with having the best manuscript. Now she found her next step. It's where she should have begun. A close analysis of the manuscript she penned reveals fissures in the perfection that had laid on these pages in the digitized letters on the screen. If this writer expected to be well published, she had also best be well edited.

Laying out the papers, the novelist reads them line by line looking for the next steps amongst what she already knows. Rejection letters are matched with companies, then companies to editors, and editors to freelancers. If the writer isn't mistaken, she has formulated a plan to email a reputable and professional editor. Jittery, yes, but she composes an email with her fingers crossed for a hopeful shot in the dark.

Unlike those letters weighing down the desk, a response comes back, affirming the availability for a discussion that could break this case wide open. This could be the call that makes the difference between publishing and waiting.

The editor's greeting puts the writer at ease, and the words flow. The novelist has found an ally in the scary uncertainty of publication. As elusive as the perpetrator of this case is to catch and lock down for the novelist, this is a true step toward the rest. At the end of the conversation, the editor throws in a plot twist. The soon-to-be author isn't as close to the mystery's solution as she thought.

The editor asks about the cover. Back to the drawing board and the Indy groups. It is time to canvas those the scribe has come across to find the one person that can place the last piece. A cover designer will be the last stop before publishing. A last-minute anonymous message on a cover designer's whereabouts saves the day.

Cover design is downtown on the corner of DIY and Help Needed Street. You can do a web search through Fiverr or Upwork for reasonably priced cover designers or design the cover yourself through any number of software packages. Now there are clear decisions to be made:

- Choose editors to review the book including a developmental editor, line editor, and proofreader.
- Work on cover design or pay someone else to design the cover.
- Understand each platform's distribution and how they handle royalties.
- Determine which platform is best for this self-publishing journey: Amazon (KDP), Lulu, IngramSpark, Barnes and Noble (Nook), or others.
- Decide on securing your own ISBN or going with the platform's assigned numbers.
- Register your book with the Library of Congress.

With those decisions made and actions ready to be taken, the writer is now face-to-face with the end result that the crescent paper stacks couldn't provide. The caper is almost finished, just one small click, and the book is born. Publishing belongs to the writer after years of writing, and months of querying, and soon, with the click of a button, a book is published!

What this sillily-told mystery of publishing a story tried to explain in an entertaining manner is that self-publishing doesn't have to be some scary place where you are left alone. Self-publishing is an avenue for freedom, to get your story out there. It allows the writer to tell their stories, to have those stories live in the world, and to be in control of the entire writing process.

Top 10 Countdown for What You Need to Self-Publish

10. A finished manuscript

9. Beta readers to even out your manuscript and make sure your audience likes the novel you have written

8. Proofread

- Developmental
- Line
- Proofreader

7. A book cover designer. If you want to be fancy, you can hire a photographer and book cover models to give you that truly original feel.

6. You may want to hire a formatter to make sure your manuscript looks correct in all formats where it is sold.

5. An ISBN or ASIN for eBooks

4. Register the book with the Library of Congress.

3. Choose your platform for self-publication and distribution.

2. Thoroughly vet all your professionals before using the services to avoid scams and ensure their credibility.

1. Enjoy being a published author and celebrate it.

Meet Wilnona Marie

Wilnona is an, are awarded poet and member of The *And I Thought Ladies*. The *And I Thought Ladies* also have novels in romance, women's fiction, and noire mystery.

She is a co-founder of 25 Hottest Authors Magazine & The And I Thought Literary Magazine, as well as the Thoughtful Book Festival. In early 2020 they served as judges on the scholastics writing and arts award.

The pair have turned their writing career into a media empire. Ranging from the written word to starring a reality show about authors which aired on channel 18 in four markets, as well as Amazon. They are principals in the Documentary

Create, Aspire, and Inspire as well as How to Become a Lady? These shows share a place under the AITL umbrella along side the four podcast and the Inspirational Women in Literature Media and Journalism Awards.

A Tale of Two Tales
William J. McGee

Lessons Learned from Traditional Publishing About Self-Publishing

Talk about not judging a book by its cover. In the case of my two books, *Attention All Passengers* and *Half the Child*, on the surface, they have very little in common. The first is a non-fiction exposè, traditionally published by HarperCollins; the second is an adult literary novel self-published by CreateSpace, the former subsidiary of Amazon.

However, I like to believe that both books have much more in common than they may appear. I not only write both fiction and non-fiction, but for ten years, I also taught both genres at the undergraduate and graduate levels. For me, the two categories meld together much more naturally than some would have you believe; and at times, I've indulged in the literary tradition of intentionally blurring the lines a bit between fiction and nonfiction. When I was in the two-year MFA program at Columbia University, my concentration was Fiction, yet my mentor (who served as the thesis advisor for my novel) was a Creative Non-fiction professor. So when all else fails, a Mark Twain quote can provide further clarification. My favorite speaks directly to this phenomenon: "Truth is stranger than fiction, but it is because fiction is obliged to stick to possibilities; truth isn't." Amen, Sam.

Both of my books have truly been labors of love for me to research, write, and promote. (Yes, novels require research, too, at least for those of us who have OCD.) But what I'm truly grateful for was having the experience of publishing via HarperCollins first before I attempted to become my own amateur publisher. That journey with professionals in the book industry gave me a very strong sense of what I needed to accomplish on my own once I decided to self-publish *Half the Child*. What I learned from the bottom up is that there are benefits and drawbacks to both methods of publishing, and subsequently, there are lessons learned that I'm eager to share.

My efforts to promote and sell both books required a personal commitment of time (including taking time off from my day job), energy (and the energies of those close to me), and capital (much more money in the case of self-publishing). But I believe those investments paid real dividends for both books, and I'm eternally grateful to my family and friends for all they've done and continue to do to assist in this work.

What follows are my top tips, which I can assure you were forged from hard-won experience and quite a bit of trial-and-error.

Focus on the cover art.

There simply is no overestimating how critical a cover can be to a book's success. As the BBC recently noted: "Everything about a book's cover—the font, the images, the colours—tells us something about what we can expect to find, or not, inside." (www.bbc.com/culture/article/20200604-the-best-book-covers-in-history) And yet, for some self-published authors, cover art is a low priority, even an afterthought. I would argue such thinking is a grave mistake, regardless of the book's content.

It is important to note that if your book is being released by a professional publisher—particularly one of the larger ones—then the cost of obtaining first-rate artists and photographers will be absorbed by the company. You'll also have the added benefit of working with industry professionals. However, if you're self-publishing, you will need to assume the costs of hiring such artists, as you may lack the skills and expertise to properly commission such work.

I simply cannot stress enough that anyone who is self-publishing should seriously consider hiring a good and talented professional artist to create the artwork. This includes not only the cover itself but the back cover and spine of the book, as well. In addition, a good artist will provide the author with titles and/or images sized for different media of varying lengths, widths, and sizes. These can be used for posters, banners, bookmarks, postcards, coffee mugs, T-shirts, baseball caps, etc. No one without vast experience in doing such sizing should even attempt to try it.

Don't skimp on page design.

As I learned on the job, there is much more to the aesthetics of book publishing than just the cover. With traditional publishing, the page size, page color, page numbering, chapter headings, the small illustrations throughout the layout, the font, font size, and the length of the bookbinding itself was all decided for me. And even if I had been asked, I would have had very little in the way of constructive input to provide.

With self-publishing, I had to take a crash course in book design. And I also had the advantage of my son's assistance, since, at the time, he was a graduate student in Architecture and was quite an expert with AutoCAD and other online design software. In this way, he was able to ensure that the interior of the novel was as clean and professional as the exterior. Page layout and design may be an afterthought for many self-published writers, but a poorly-designed book is a sure sign that the author cut corners, and it can subliminally give a reader the sense that this work is NOT of professional quality. This can bleed over into how they evaluate the writing itself. Nothing says amateur like a "widow"—that one lonely word on a line or one lonely sentence on a page.

Developmental editing and copyediting are critical!

Okay, enough about how all those pages LOOK. The focus of a book, of course, is the content itself—the writing. And just as lawyers who represent themselves have fools for clients, authors who edit themselves have fools for readers.

With traditional publishing, this isn't a worry because you'll likely have an agent, at least one editor, and other publishing professionals who will weigh in during the process. But editing can be a problem for self-published authors, particularly if they're unsure where to turn and whom to trust with the early drafts of their work.

I've been lucky over the years to have cultivated a small yet trustworthy cadre of authors whom I can rely on to provide brutally honest criticism of my work. And I do the same for them because we are of the like mind that lying to a professional writer about their work is the opposite of kindness—it's actually quite harmful. My group includes ex-classmates, fellow Creative Writing teachers, or simply friends I've picked up along the way, but all have been professionally published. And I entrusted them with early readings of *Half the Child* to address any and all big-picture developmental issues. I've found that this is an overlooked step in the self-publishing process of many writers, and quite frankly, it can show in the finished product.

Equally true is the critical role of a good copyeditor for the necessary line editing. Now although I have never technically been a copyeditor myself, as a writing professor and a journalist who has been both a Managing Editor and an Editor-in-Chief, copyediting was always intrinsic to my work in these fields. So by the time *Half the Child* was ready for copyediting, I was convinced this was a mere formality because I had signed off on as "clean" a manuscript as any editor could hope to read. Wow, was I wrong.

At least I was smart enough to retain the best, my friend Lynne Bernstein, who has years of copyediting experience and as fine an editor's "eye" as I've ever encountered. When we first met many years ago, she was a copyeditor on the news desk for the Associated Press in New York City's Rockefeller Center, and it's hard to imagine a more stressful and time-sensitive gig for an editor. But Lynne shone at AP, and she shone with my novel. So imagine my shock when she sent back my "clean" manuscript with pages and pages of valid edits! I learned then and there never to underestimate the importance of a second (or third) set of eyes on my work.

Copyediting often reveals two common types of errors: 1) simple mistakes that the author just didn't catch and 2) inconsistencies from one page to another. Such inconsistencies can be wide-ranging because two or more styles are perfectly acceptable—but not in the same book! So, is it ok or okay (or o.k. or O.K.?) Is it the army or the Army? Is it 5 o'clock or five o'clock? Is it am/pm or AM/PM? You get the idea. If you think that just grammar Nazis or the OCD-afflicted are the only ones who notice such inconsistencies, you're wrong. Even readers who don't consciously process such errors can intrinsically sense that a book has not been properly edited.

Those who are traditionally published rarely have to worry about this. But those with self-published books are squarely responsible for avoiding such problems.

Invest in public relations.

Professionally promoting your work is a must.

My traditionally-published *Attention All Passengers* was launched in late June 2012, which turned out to be a masterstroke of great luck as the book chronicled the inherent problems with America's broken commercial air service. Airlines tend to experience their worst service problems during the summer months, and I wound up logging more than 50 media appearances in the first few weeks. A HarperCollins publicist assisted me with a full hour on NPR's *Fresh Air*, CNN (twice), FOX News, and a marathon, early morning, four-hour series of radio tapings that started with stations on the East Coast and went clear across the Pacific Ocean.

So with traditional publishing, I had the best of both worlds: I was assisted by a professional book publicist, but I also supplemented it with my own efforts, including writing an op-ed on airline safety that ran in *The New York Times* just prior to publication. And all of this, of course, was my training school for self-publishing several years later.

With my second book, I invested in the professional assistance of an expert, and, I retained my friend Les Luchter, who is a professional public relations consultant. The very first thing he did was read *Half the Child*, which may sound obvious but is not; you'd be amazed how many publicists promote work they're personally unfamiliar with themselves.

Les was able to do what I and all other authors cannot successfully do for ourselves: Speak about our books in the highest possible terms. I assure you, when it comes to promotion, third-person ("You'll love her/his/their book") works MUCH better than first-person ("I may be the best living American novelist, if I do say myself"). He also created and distributed press releases, synopses, and artwork, and distributed it to media in key regions, such as Connecticut, where I live, and Queens, where the novel is set. Even though *Half the Child* was self-published, Les was instrumental in securing favorable publicity for me in those crucial early days and weeks after publication.

Les and I also worked together to focus our energies on various forms of media outlets, including:

- Print media, such as traditional newspapers, magazines, and journals
- blogs and other online sites
- Radio and TV programs
- Podcasts

Of these, blogs and podcasts may be most unfamiliar to some authors, and yet in my view, they also offer some of the finest opportunities. I've had the good fortune to promote my work before audiences as large as CNN's, and yet in terms of actually reaching the targeted readers of my books, I've found that blogs and podcasts can be best. That's because they both can be quite specific in their topics of discussion, affording you the perfect audience for your work.

For those who are being traditionally published, it's critical to understand exactly what—AND WHAT NOT—your publisher will be doing to promote your book. But for those embarking on the self-publishing journey, the onus will be entirely on you. And to paraphrase the old axiom: You'll never get a second chance to make a first impression with your book launch.

• • •

Embrace media appearances.

I get it—writers are often not the best public speakers. In fact, writers often ARE writers precisely because they are not public speakers. So asking some writers to embrace media appearances is like asking a fish to embrace a trapeze. But I can assure you that I've seen immediate results from public appearances, and by this, I mean I've witnessed the sales of my books take an immediate upward turn.

First things first: What exactly is your work, and who exactly is your audience? Or, more accurately, who CAN BE part of your audience? Those are critical questions, and they can be instrumental in helping you promote your book.

Take my novel *Half the Child*. At its core, it's a story of a devoted father who puts every aspect of his life on hold in fighting to remain in his young son's life during a traumatic custody and abduction drama, all due to a syndrome that some mental health and legal professionals have labeled Parental Alienation. Therefore, this brief summary identifies numerous potential topics of interest to certain readers:

- fathers
- parents
- children
- families
- marriage
- divorce
- custody
- abduction
- Parental Alienation

But the wonderful thing about a novel is that it allows both writer and reader to explore not just the primary world of the subject matter, but dozens of other secondary and tertiary worlds, as well. Consider that *Half the Child* is set almost entirely in the New York City borough of Queens. And that Michael Mullen, the novel's narrator and protagonist, is from a large (but loud and loving) Irish-American family. And Michael is an air traffic controller at LaGuardia Airport, as well as an Air Force veteran. And he's enrolled part-time in graduate school at New York University studying Psychology. And in his spare time, he's a member of a boxing gym. And despite his trauma, during the course of the novel, he ventures back into the dating world and even flirts with romance. Now scroll upward and realize just how many reader demographics can successfully intersect with one or even many of these components of a single novel.

Once I identified potential readers, then it was easier to target prospective buyers of the book. For example, I reached out to air traffic control organizations to promote *Half the Child*, and I also reached out to boxing gyms. But it was in the burgeoning fields of fathers' rights and Parental Alienation that I gained the most traction. Shortly after the novel was published, I sent copies to the heads of the Parental Alienation Study Group (PASG), the world's leading medical, legal, and academic authority on this topic; they correctly noted that while there were numerous nonfiction books and textbooks on the subject, *Half the Child* seemed to be the first novel to take on PA directly. That led to a series of podcasts and personal reading appearances and culminated when I gave a keynote address at PASG's global conference in Philadelphia in 2019. I read from and spoke about my novel before some 200 people who all had personal experience with the painful topic of PA. That day, I established lasting relationships and was able to share my book with dozens of new readers. And it all came because I embraced speaking publicly about the novel. And this was all the more critical because *Half the Child* was self-published. Because if I hadn't taken the initiative, who would have?

Build a dedicated website.

That term "homepage" is oh so apt. That's how I view the website for *Half the Child* (www.HalfTheChild.com). It's the home not only for my novel but really for my work itself. It's the space from which everything else flows, and it's the best way for anyone to learn more about my writing. When I'm speaking to someone and they have questions about the novel, or they would like to invite me to a reading, or they simply want to know the best way to buy my books, all I need to do is suggest they visit the website.

Awards, endorsements, blurbs, reviews, photos, news, synopses, upcoming events…all this and more can be added to the website. And all of it can continually be updated and revised, as well. A good website simultaneously offers both permanence and immediacy.

Of course, every good website should have a contact page, and that's why I created a dedicated email account that is linked to my website. It's the easiest method for prospective readers and all other interested parties to reach out to you. And it's also a way for strangers and the general public to contact you without violating the privacy of your own personal email accounts. Trust me—this is critically important if you're interacting in public forums.

I know, I know—but give social media a try.

In the 2020s, more than ever, the charm of social media has worn off, and many Americans have signed off—for good. Privacy concerns, political spats, frustrations over pop-up advertising, disagreements with the owners of sites such as Facebook or Twitter, and many more issues have spurred users to shut down their pages. But here's the thing: Social media can be a tremendous source of both publicity and sales for a new book or even an established book that's been out in the world for a while. And it can be a relatively inexpensive form of advertising.

For *Half the Child*, I maintain separate social media accounts (in addition to my own personal or work-related accounts) on Facebook, Twitter, LinkedIn, Instagram, TikTok, and YouTube. Each of these sites is different from the others, and those differences are exemplified in tone, style, language, visuals, audience, etc. If I'm planning a reading, for example, I will post about it on all these platforms (as well as on the novel's website), but I'll tweak things a bit from site to site. LinkedIn is more professional, while Facebook is a little more chatty. Twitter is truncated and punchy like a billboard. Instagram is all about the visual image, while TikTok is all about the moving image. YouTube allows for lengthier video discussions. Demographically, I'm reaching different audiences, so of course, my message will differ a bit even though the product remains the same.

I track the sales myself via Amazon—and I track them fairly closely. So I can see an almost immediate bang for my buck when I invest time and sometimes even money in social media. I've learned, for example, that a modest outlay of targeted ads on Facebook can produce better results than the same amount spent on Amazon itself, where most of the actual purchases are transacted. I can target an audience based on gender, age, marital status, geographical location, etc. For example, because *Half the Child* chronicles the love and devotion of a young dad, I can use social media to target parents of both genders in the weeks before Father's Day.

Traditionally-published authors were able to leave such promotion to others. But now, even the largest book publishers will tell authors, as HarperCollins told me, that you must do more promoting than writers did in the past. Therefore, I believe self-published authors who are not on social media are doing themselves tremendous harm. You don't need to live for hours every day online, and you don't need to engage those with whom you don't want to interact. But updates about the big events in the life of your book(s) are critical, and social media can be an extremely effective tool.

Consider hosting a book launch party.

Think of a launch party as your book's entrance into the world. And as with every birth, consider celebrating it and shouting it from the rooftops. It will not only fire up your enthusiasm, but undoubtedly it will do the same for others in your orbit so that they, in turn, can help promote your new book for you. Such a party could be in a bookstore, a library, an educational institution, a public space, or a private event venue. Or even in your own home or the home of a friend. Beware that when it comes to spending, book parties are like weddings—you can do it modestly or you can allow the sky to be the limit. I've been to launches in libraries and bookstores that were quite inexpensive, and I've been to lavish events that included hot buffets, open bars, and lots of giveaways and tchotchkes.

In my case, I was lucky to have two wonderful launches to welcome each of my books. For *Attention All Passengers*, I rented loft space in New York City and provided fruit, cheese, wine, and beer. It was a little high for my budget, but I was treating myself more than my guests because I had fantasized for so long about having my first book published that I wanted to mark the event in a big way. And we all certainly did.

For *Half the Child*, I was very lucky. Although the novel is NOT about the airline industry like *Attention All Passengers*, the book does, in fact, have a strong aviation connection as the fictional narrator/protagonist, Michael Mullen, is an air traffic controller at New York's LaGuardia Airport. Well, as luck would have it, I happened to have taught (and continue to lecture) at one of the leading aeronautical colleges in the United States. And that institution—Vaughn College of Aeronautics—not only is located directly adjacent to LaGuardia Airport, but it even offers a program of study for students training to become air traffic controllers. The president and faculty of the college were kind enough to host the launch of *Half the Child*, and my many guests were able to mingle in the giant atrium and even pay visits to the mock control tower on the roof of the school. It was a memorable kick-off to one of the only novels ever written from the perspective of an air traffic controller.

Both achievements were very important to me: my first published book and my first novel going out into the world. I wanted to celebrate these occasions. But I also wanted to rally the troops so that those close to me could celebrate, as well—and celebrate the books. Dozens and dozens of friends and relatives posted photos and tributes of these parties on social media, which in turn led to more publicity and more sales. Depending on your budget, a launch party can be money very well spent.

Never stop giving readings.

It's really that simple. Unlike some products that can go out of style, a good book can live on and on, so that authors can continue to share it with new audiences. And the best way to share it is through personal appearances—the readings and discussions that I love participating in so much. In any given month, I'll be reading from *Half the Child* at a bookstore, a library, a college, or a professional organization. Even chain bookstores such as Barnes and Noble welcome local authors, as do community organizations that take pride in homegrown talent. And libraries can be a great source for new authors as well.

At my readings, I bring oversized posters of both my book covers, as well as hand-outs—*Half the Child* bookmarks and postcards—and usually treats such as candy. I've been lucky enough to have my large family assist, so that my son often takes over processing the sales of the books I'm reading from, while my sisters have hosted readings in locations as far away as Virginia Beach and Buffalo.

Will a traditional publisher assist you in such readings? It's possible, but unlikely. So both traditional and self-published authors must teach themselves—ALWAYS BE READING! Always. For a book to stay alive, you must ensure there's always a new stream of readers just waiting to be introduced to it.

Book clubs are your friends.

I've saved book clubs for last because, in many ways, they're my favorite way to discuss my writing. Usually, they're rather intimate, but I have read before clubs with 30 or more people. Often there's a connection, so I know at least one of the members (although I'm perfectly happy to appear before book clubs hosted by strangers). But most of all, there is a shared bond from all of us having read the same work, and—regardless of whether the feedback is positive, negative, or neutral—this familiarity creates a level of closeness.

When you read from a book that people have not yet bought, let alone read, you're acting at least in part as a sales representative, and many authors are not always totally comfortable in that role. Even among the most devout bibliophiles, a book represents a financial investment, and at some bookstore readings, I can almost see my listeners weighing whether or not I have convinced them to make a purchase. All that tension is erased at book clubs because the sales took place long ago, and now the focus is on enjoying the work itself.

And from an author's perspective, there's another big advantage to book club readings and discussions. In the case of *Half the Child*, the plot is so complex and fast-moving that I'm effectively unable to read much past the first 50 pages or so without issuing spoiler alerts and giving away critical plot points. With book clubs, all the members have already read the novel, so I have the pleasure of reading sections that I could never read to an audience of newcomers. In fact, at book clubs, I often ask the members if they would like to suggest a section or two for me to read so that we can all share their favorite passages.

So which is better for an author, the power of being represented by a well-known book publisher or the autonomy of self-publishing to your own personal specifications? Each has its advantages. But to me, the similarities far outweigh the differences. The key is for the writer to take an active involvement in the life of their book. And that can be tremendous fun, as well.

For more marketing ideas and to dig deeper into the marketing topics discussed in this chapter, read *Launch Pad: The Countdown to Marketing Your Book*.

Top 10 Countdown to Publishing Success

10. Focus on the cover art.

9. Don't skimp on page design.

8. Developmental editing and copyediting are critical!

7. Invest in public relations.

6. Embrace media appearances.

5. Build a dedicated website.

4. I know, I know—but give social media a try.

3. Consider hosting a book launch party.

2. Never stop giving readings.

1. Book clubs are your friends.

Meet William J. McGee

McGee was born in New York City and received an MFA in Fiction from Columbia University. Among other pursuits, he represents travelers as a consumer advocate for American Economic Liberties Project; taught undergraduate and graduate Creative Writing for ten years; worked in airline flight operations management; served in the US Air Force Auxiliary; and was an award-winning investigative journalist, columnist, and Editor of *Consumer Reports Travel Letter*.

He is developing *AirFear*, a scripted television drama. McGee lives in Connecticut and is also a father.

www.HalfTheChild

Afterword

What a journey we are on as authors! We spend our days rearranging 26 letters on a computer screen in the hope of creating worlds in which others long to be. We edit and rewrite and reimagine our stories all in order to, exhausted and triumphantly, type the words "the end." But since you have joined us here for *Launch Pad: The Countdown to Publishing Your Book* we know that for you writing the book is only part of the story. To feel complete as an author you must publish and place this creation of yours out in the world.

What I have learned over the years is that writers need to write and true authors need to publish. This is my sixth book. I have worked with the full gamut of publishing options. Some have been easy, and some have been hard. Very hard. But I will tell you that regardless of the path, there is no feeling equal to the moment when your book shows up in your hands, has a cover that you love, and has your name across that cover. Publishing is the goal of authors, a goal as tangible as the hopes of Pinocchio or the Velveteen Rabbit to become real. When your book is "real," the world changes.

If I have a hallmark for my work life, it is creative collaborations, and this endeavor is no different. This book grew out of a confluence of experiences. Each of my books has changed my life direction in some way. However, none more so than my novel *The Eves*. There had been a multi-year gap between my publications, a pandemic, and I was publishing fiction for the first time. The world of publishing changed and I changed. The launch of *The Eves* led me to seek and find great collaborations within the reading-writing community. One of those collaborations was with the Facebook group *Bookish Road Trip*, another was with Authors on the Air Global Radio Network, and a third was with Red Penguin Books. Here, I met, respectively Mary Helen Sheriff, Pam Stack, and Stephanie Larkin. You'll meet Mary in book three of our series on marketing. Like many authors, after the launch of *The Eves,* I grew to expand my author life to include multiple platforms to share my voice. I became Director of Membership for *Bookish Road* Trip, launched an author speaker's group called *Author Talk Network*, published an eBook with Red Penguin Books, and created a radio show called *The Storytellers*.

As it tends to happen, one thing led to another. Mary decided to start an author marketing coach business. I was fascinated by all she shared, and, quite frankly, all I didn't know when I went to launch *The Eves*. I approached Mary with the idea of collaborating on a combination of a radio show and marketing support that would celebrate book releases and the authors that create them. She was a yes! I approached Pam Stack, the brilliant and supportive owner of Authors on the Air, and asked what she thought of me hosting a second show on the network. Yes! *Launch Pad* the radio show and marketing experience was born! While Mary and I were still in the planning stages for the show, the first season filled with guests. The Season Two line-up was complete after our first episode aired. As we go to press, we have a twenty-person guest waiting list. We were on to something.

Authors need support in launching their books. Indeed, we benefit from a supportive collaboration in writing, publishing, and marketing our work.

When I saw *Launch Pad* the radio show, take off, so to speak, I circled back to Mary and suggested the idea of this book series with Mary taking the lead on the marketing volume. Yes! I then reached out to Scotland-based book coach Emma Dhesi and asked if she would be interested in leading a book on writing. Yes! Lastly, I approached Stephanie, Red Penguin's CEO.

"So, Stephanie, I have this idea for a book series—three books, on craft, publishing, and marketing, modeled after my radio show *Launch Pad*, supports to authors . . . I've got lead authors for books one and three and think you should do book two on publishing. What do you think?"

Stephanie will tell you, in her 17 years as a publisher, it's the fastest "yes" she has ever said.

Eight months after I approached Mary, Emma, and Stephanie, *Launch Pad: The Countdown to Writing, Publishing, and Marketing Your Book* became real.

We wrote this book to help make your world change, to help *your* book become real.

For many, as Zibby Owens so honestly and beautifully starts this book out, getting to publication can be a rejection-filled multi-year journey to finding an agent and/or publisher. Others will find quicker, easier paths through skill and through luck. Still, others will find shorter paths with self-publishing and hybrid presses.

In this volume, we've aimed to provide you with deep insights and credible tools that will help you navigate your publishing journey. We've brought together an amazing array of talented voices from the publishing world to help you on your way. We have also provided ways for you to learn more about their work, seek their counsel, and engage with them and their organizations. I know I have learned something from every chapter. Sarah Bullen expanded my understanding of the quest to find an agent. Robb Grindstaff honed in on the importance of exacting editing. DC Gomez opened a new world to me in her chapter on "KU vs Wide." Natalie Obando expanded my worldview and appreciation for BIPOC writers, and Theresa Bakken gave me a broad appreciation for publishing audiobooks. We took on the tasks of addressing how to best work with publishers and how to understand the business/money-making side of this work. Six publishers, each an author themself . . . Betty Lee Crosby, Christine Kloser, Erika Lance, Stephanie Larkin, Brooke Warner, and Valerie Willis . . . all generously lent their voices, experience, and expertise to these pages. I am grateful to each of them for their wisdom and for so generously giving their time and talents to this collaboration. *They* have made this book real.

Throughout this volume, you have read individual perspectives, opinions, and even writing styles. Together we are so proud of this work. We thank you for visiting with us here and invite you to expand your reading with the other two books in our series. We wish you every success, invite you to contact us, and celebrate your publishing accomplishments.

Writers write. Authors publish.

Sarasota, Florida
April 2023

Find out more about Grace and her work at:

Website: www.GraceSammon.Net
Facebook: https://www.facebook.com/GraceSammonWrites/
Instagram: https://www.instagram.com/GraceSammonWrites/

Next Steps

We are so excited to join you on your writing journey. For more free resources and downloads, please visit:

https://launchpadcountdown.com/downloads-2/

Enter the password: LaunchPadPublishing.

Be sure to grab your copy of:

Available Now   Available June 20, 2023

Available wherever books are sold.